AURA

RAPIDLY ENHANCE YOUR EXECUTIVE PRESENCE

SUMIT SAHNI

ISBN
Paperback: 979-8-89519-529-1
Hardcase: 979-8-89544-877-9

Contents

Part 1

Understanding AURA and Executive Presence

AURA - Executive Presence

Steve Jobs, the legendary co-founder of Apple Inc., was known for his remarkable aura and executive presence. One notable instance that showcased his exceptional executive presence was the introduction and launch of iCloud during an event.

At the time of the iCloud launch, most people were unaware of the power of cloud, and they were used to a tiring process of transferring data from their phones to Mac. Apple's iCloud aimed to solve this problem by linking all devices to the cloud so that data could be seamlessly transferred automatically.

Jobs' keynote presentation would play a crucial role in conveying the vision and potential of this ground-breaking innovation.

During this presentation, Jobs did the following:

Displayed Empathy

During the keynote, Jobs demonstrated high levels of customer empathy by sharing the problem from the customer's perspective. He used powerful imagery to help the audience understand the problem that the innovation was looking to solve.

Compelling Storytelling

Jobs employed the power of storytelling to engage his audience. He converted a tough technical topic like iCloud into a compelling story by sharing the problem statement, how Apple was planning to solve it, and the benefits that iCloud will give to the customers. This clever narrative technique not only captured the audience's imagination but also set the stage for a successful launch of the product.

Powerful Visuals

Jobs' presentation was crafted to maximize the impact of his message. He utilized powerful visuals while explaining the problem. While explaining the iCloud, he showed an image of how Apple was demoting Mac and replacing it with iCloud to become the hub for all devices. He displayed how data will flow from one device to iCloud and eventually be transmitted to other devices. His confident presentation left a lasting impression on the audience.

Distinctive Language and Messaging:

Jobs employed concise and impactful language to articulate the value proposition of the iCloud. Phrases such as "next big insight", "digital hub for digital life", and "everything works automatically" were strategically used to convey the transformative impact on the lives of customers. Jobs' messaging not only created excitement but also instilled confidence in Apple's ability to deliver on its promises.

Audience Engagement

While delivering the keynote, Jobs engaged the audience by incorporating moments of humor. He shared the problem statement in a humorous manner and also spoke about past failed innovations by Apple. This not only engaged the audience but also built confidence that Apple was learning and adapting.

This story, and many such instances, have contributed to Jobs' image as an innovative leader.

We can certainly mention that Jobs had an AURA around him, and his executive presence went a long way in building this aura.

In a dictionary, aura is defined as "a distinctive atmosphere or quality that seems to surround and be generated by a person." This definition underlines the meaning and importance of executive presence.

Executive presence is not just about communicating with impact. Communication is just the input of executive presence. Executive presence is more about generating an output, which is the aura.

Output from the perspective of aura means answering 2 questions:

1. How do listeners feel about the communicator during and at the end of communication?

2. How do listeners feel about themselves during and after the communication?

Therefore, that way, I like to define executive presence as:

Executive presence is the ability of a leader to generate an aura, inspire confidence, and influence effectively. This happens with the leader's ability to command attention, demonstrate authenticity, gravitas, and poise.

Why does executive presence matter?

Let's look at the story of John (name changed):

John was a diligent and hardworking business executive. From a young age, John had shown a remarkable aptitude for strategic thinking, problem-solving, and a tireless work ethic. He excelled in execution.

John quickly climbed the corporate ladder, securing a mid-level management position in a prominent company. His technical skills and dedication to his work were well recognized and admired by his colleagues and superiors.

However, as the years went by, John began to notice a disturbing pattern. Despite his impressive track record, he found it hard to convince his stakeholders on new ideas. His ability to inspire confidence was weak, and he could see that because of this, his career growth had hit a plateau.

John sought feedback from his mentors, and it was during one such conversation that he received a surprising insight: his lack of executive presence was holding him back!

People felt that John struggled to assert his ideas confidently, communicate with impact, and command the attention of his colleagues and higher-ups. For example, when he facilitated business planning meetings, he was focusing only on the numbers and found it hard to communicate complex messages in a simple manner. His team felt that business planning meetings with John were more information sessions, and they didn't come out of that feeling "charged up."

Since John was so focused on execution, he had never realized that executive presence was such a critical capability!

The corporate world has many leaders like John who are extremely sincere leaders with a strong set of strategic thinking, problem-solving, and execution capabilities. Like in John's case, these capabilities serve them well in the early part of their careers. However, many such leaders lack the aura, and they find themselves hitting the glass ceiling early.

Several of these leaders tend to discount the importance of executive presence by making statements like, "my work will prove my worth" or "eventually, people will see my value." While these feelings are natural for any sincere leader to have, they can also serve as a block to learning executive presence and accelerating their growth.

Additionally, several researchers have underlined the importance of executive presence. Here are some key points supported by research:

- **Leadership Perception:** Studies have shown that executive presence significantly influences how leaders are perceived by their superiors, peers, and subordinates. A research study by Gentry et al. (2016) found that executive presence accounted for 26% of the variance in overall leadership effectiveness ratings.

- **Career Advancement:** Research suggests that executive presence plays a significant role in career advancement. A study by Hewlett et al. (2014) found that senior leaders often attributed their success to their ability to project confidence, build relationships, and communicate effectively, which are key components of executive presence.

- **Influence and Decision-Making:** Executive presence enhances a leader's ability to influence others and make strategic decisions. Research by Derue et al. (2011) showed that leaders with high executive presence were more likely to be seen as persuasive and credible, thus increasing their impact on decision-making processes within their organizations.

- **Team Performance:** Executive presence also has a positive impact on team performance. A study conducted by Bono and Judge (2004) found that leaders with high executive presence were more likely to create an environment of trust, motivation, and commitment among team members, resulting in improved team performance and productivity.

In summary, spending time developing your executive presence is an investment with a very high rate of return!

AURA Model

Former President of India, the late Dr. A.P.J Abdul Kalam, was one of the most inspiring global leaders of modern times. Dr. Kalam had an aura about him; whenever he spoke, the entire nation was spellbound and listened to him.

While his achievements were far beyond, the fact that he had an inspiring presence, we can certainly also learn executive presence from him.

For those of us who have had a chance to listen to him, if we close our eyes and imagine Dr. Kalam speaking, many things will come to our mind.

One of the key things that made Dr. Kalam special was his very character. Even after accomplishing so much, Dr. Kalam was a very humble and down-to-earth leader. He had no air or arrogance surrounding him, and his presence inspired humility in others. Dr. Kalam also had a strong depth in the subjects he spoke about. You could notice his subject matter strength based on the words, examples, and analogies he used to describe his ideas.

The other inspiring character trait of Dr. Kalam was his dedication. Whether as the President of India or previously as Chief Scientific Adviser to the Prime Minister, Dr. Kalam performed all his roles with steadfast dedication.

As a speaker, Dr. Kalam was equally inspiring! His messages were always well-structured, and he communicated in a precise manner. For example, during one of his speeches to the students of IIT Madras, Dr. Kalam communicated in a very logical manner the key pain points for youth in India and followed it up with some very practical and inspirational advice.

As a speaker, the way he communicated evoked positive emotions in others. He frequently used inclusive language, stories, and pauses in his presentations to engage his listeners. He was naturally able to modulate his voice to keep people at the edge of their seats!

Here is a short note on a part of his speech at IIT Madras:

- During the early part of his speech, Dr. Kalam shared that he has interacted with more than 11 million youth, and they all are dealing with one common challenge: "How to be unique as an individual."

- He then explained to the group that while everyone wants to be unique, the world around wants everyone to behave in the same manner.

- Then he asked a question to the audience, "Do you want to be unique or like everybody else?" To this, he got a resounding answer from the audience that they wanted to be unique.

- He then shared four tools to be unique as an individual. These were:

  o Setting the goal

  o Acquiring knowledge

  o Hard work and devotion.

  o Perseverance

During the entire speech, he continued to make strong logical connections and evoke emotions of the audience.

As we reflect on the above, we realize that his aura was magnetic because of three key things:

- **Character Traits:** Dr. Kalam, as a person, was unique and inspiring. His strong, but humble, character was inspiring to people.

- **Cognitive Confidence:** As a speaker, Dr. Kalam was very logical and structured. Additionally, he was precise in his articulation.

- **Evoking Emotions:** The way Dr. Kalam spoke, he evoked emotions in others.

AURA Framework

During my consulting career, I have had the chance to observe and interact with several leaders who have an aura. I have been able to observe them closely and study the concept of executive presence. I have noticed that the aura of the person depends on 3 aspects:

Who they are:

Leaders with a strong aura and executive presence display 3-character strengths. I like to call them the 3Ds - Depth, Dedication, and Down to Earth. These character strengths serve as magnets for them.

How They Think and Articulate:

Leaders with strong executive presence are logical thinkers. Their clarity of mind is visible when they communicate. However, apart from being logical thinkers, their articulation is precise. They don't "over-talk" or "over-deliver."

Precisely because of this potent combination of logical thinking and precise articulation, they are able to build "cognitive confidence" with others. Cognitive confidence means the individual's ability to inspire confidence by the way they frame their thoughts.

How They Evoke Emotions Through Communication:

Leaders with aura are also able to evoke emotions of their listeners by deploying engaging communication methods. They are able to inspire their audience through a combination of techniques like storytelling, inclusive language, metaphors, voice modulation, among many others.

The aura framework given below provides a broad introduction to each of these aspects. You will notice several tools and techniques that I will cover in greater detail.

In this book, I would be covering each of these 3 aspects of the AURA model in detail. My attempt is to share some very practical examples, techniques, and methods so that you can rapidly enhance your executive presence.

Though character traits are the core, deliberately, I will be covering them at the end. This is because I will be able to communicate their power in a lot more precise manner once we have covered the other 2 aspects.

As you go through the material, I encourage you to take time out to reflect and apply the techniques. You will notice considerable immediate benefit in doing so!

So, lets dive in!

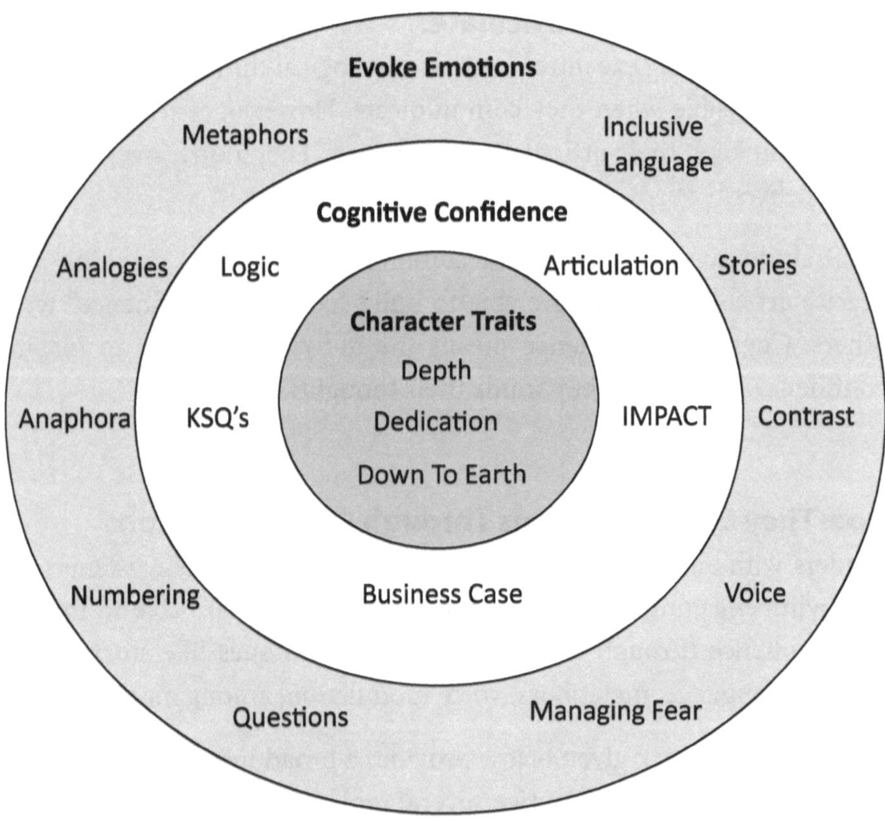

Part 2

Building Cognitive Confidence

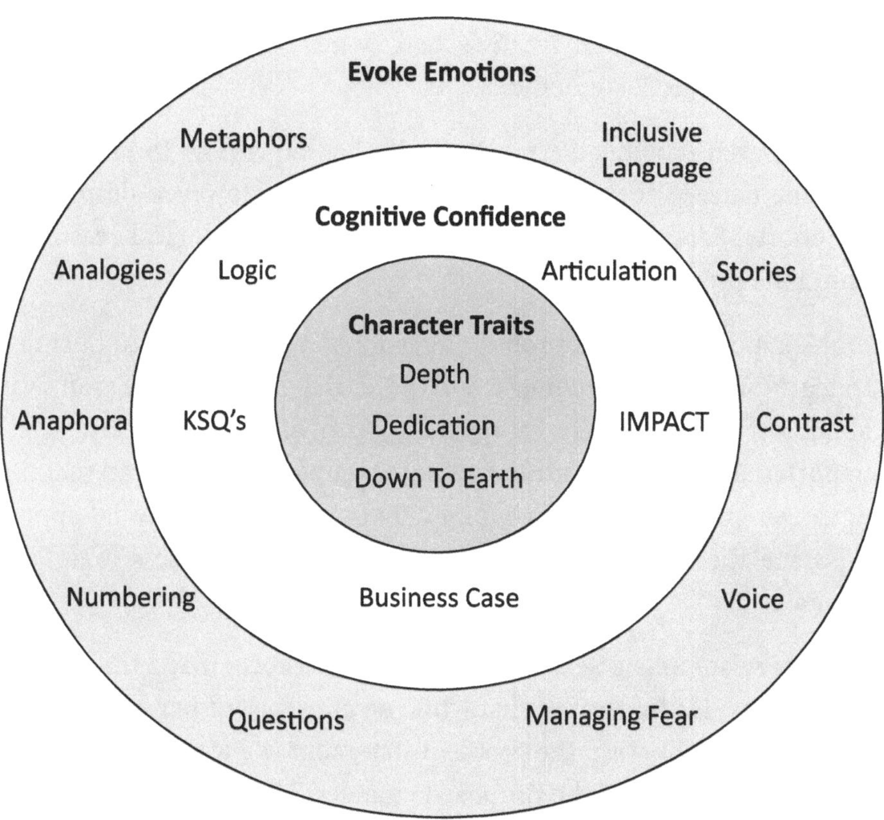

Cognitive Confidence

Let's look at 2 stories to understand the concept of cognitive confidence from 2 different perspectives.

Story 1: Sarah

Sarah was a middle manager in a large organization. She was known for her dedication and exceptional work ethic.

Sarah had a brilliant idea to streamline the company's project management process, which she believed would significantly improve efficiency and productivity. She had done thorough research and analyzed the benefits of her idea.

Excited, Sarah scheduled a meeting with her supervisor to present the idea. She entered the meeting with enthusiasm. However, despite her best efforts, Sarah struggled to clearly articulate the logical reasoning behind the proposal.

Sarah's supervisor asked probing questions about linkage to business strategy, projected outcomes, and potential challenges. Sarah was caught off guard as she struggled to provide coherent and well-supported arguments. As the meeting progressed, she started making vague statements. The meeting quickly became an emotional appeal to pursue the idea rather than an appeal to the business logic and rationale.

Her supervisor was a seasoned executive and recognized the gaps in Sarah's logic. He told Sarah that while he appreciated her enthusiasm, he could not fully grasp the problem statement she was trying to solve and the practicality of the proposed changes. He also mentioned that he was not sure whether all risks and other alternatives had been considered and suggested she refine her idea more. Sarah was really disheartened.

Story 2: Emily

Emily was a middle manager in an organization, and she was highly regarded for her exceptional logical thinking skills, analytical prowess, and attention to detail. Her ability to break down complex problems and devise practical solutions made her a valuable asset to the company.

One day, an opportunity arose for Emily to present an innovative idea to the senior leadership team.

As Emily began her presentation, her enthusiasm for the idea was visible.

However, she soon found herself talking too much and elaborating on every minor detail. She went into unnecessary tangents, losing the clarity and focus of her main message. The leadership team grew increasingly confused, struggling to grasp the core concept amidst the outpour of information.

She also repeated the same messages over and over again, which made the leadership team extremely impatient. Her sentences were long and never-ending!

Her inability to convey her ideas succinctly hindered her ability to communicate the value and feasibility of her proposal effectively. Despite her strong logical thinking skills, the audience found it challenging to connect the dots and understand the practical implications of her idea.

At the end of the presentation, she was informed that the senior leadership team was not completely convinced with her idea.

As we reflect on the 2 stories above, each of them presents a different issue. In Sarah's case, it was a lack of logical thinking behind her idea, but Emily faced a different issue altogether. For Emily, the issue was not logical thinking, but her inability to communicate in a precise manner.

These 2 stories underline the concept of cognitive confidence.

Cognitive confidence is the individual's ability to build confidence in others by showcasing logical thinking and by communicating with precision and clarity.

People who are high in building cognitive confidence make listeners feel that:

- The ideas proposed by the communicator are strong and rational.

- They can clearly understand the logical reasoning behind the idea.

- They can trust in the practicality of the proposed arguments.

- That the communicator has built confidence in them to pursue proposed ideas.

During my work with coaching business leaders, I have realized that many of them have strong ideas, but they can lack in one of the two key underlying capabilities that impact cognitive confidence:

1. Logical reasoning and/or,

2. Precise articulation.

One way of thinking about this is by reflecting on the matrix below.

On the X-axis, we have a leader's logical thinking capability, and on the Y-axis, we have their ability to articulate with precision. Effectively, there are 4 types of profiles here:

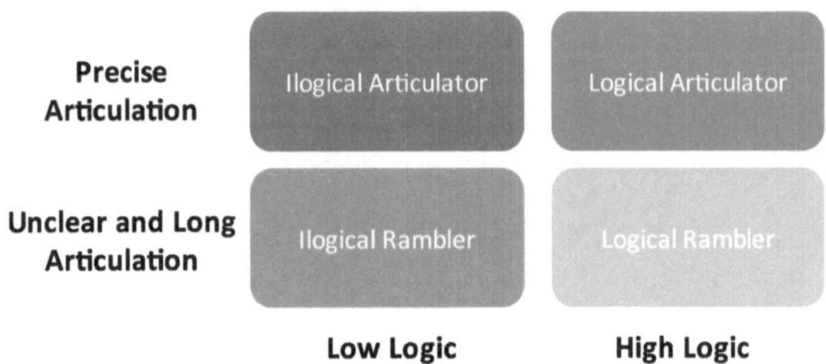

- **Illogical Articulator**: These leaders have a precise way of articulating their ideas. They can keep the communication concise; however, their ideas lack the needed logical reasoning, and therefore, they struggle to create confidence in others.

Sometimes, illogical articulators have a tendency to fall in love with one idea without doing proper research. They can be overexcited about their idea, which diminishes their capability to identify other alternatives or potential risks.

- **Logical Rambler**: Like Emily, several business leaders can be in this quadrant. They have strong logical thinking skills and rationale to support their views, however, they have a tendency to "over-deliver."

  They fall into the trap of talking too much, getting into minute details, and can fall prey to a monologue. This confuses their listeners and does not inspire confidence.

- **Illogical Rambler:** This is obviously a problematic place to be in. These leaders lack the logic in their presentation and also talk too much. As surprising as this may sound, many business leaders can be in this quadrant!

- **Logical Articulator**: People in this quadrant build cognitive confidence. They create enough confidence with their listeners as their arguments are supported with sound logic and they communicate with needed conciseness.

  Being aware of where you are as an individual in this matrix is of crucial importance. That is because lack of structure in the mind directly impacts our ability to present with impact.

Self-awareness in this area will also lead to being deliberate on creating cognitive confidence with others. Logical thinking does not guarantee precise articulation, and similarly, precise articulation does not guarantee logical thinking. As communicators, we need both!

The next page has a short self-assessment tool on the same. Take some time to do this, and let's see where you are on this framework!

Self-Assessment Tool:

Here is a quick tool for you to assess yourself on these dimensions. On the statements below, rate yourself on a scale of 1 to 5. Use 5 if you are very good in this area and 1 if you have a lot to improve on.

Dimension	Statement	Rating (1-5)
Precise Articulation.	When I communicate, my articulation is precise, and I don't repeat the same message.	
	Most people will find my communication to be crisp.	
	I stay on the topic of discussion and avoid going off in different, unrelated dimensions.	
	Most people tell me that I am very clear in communication.	
	I don't find myself needing to explain my idea repetitively.	
Logic	I find it easy to make other people understand my logic or rationale.	
	I am able to provide relevant facts and details as needed.	
	I can easily define the problem statements and why the problem needs to be solved.	
	When developing ideas, I consider multiple alternatives and carefully assess the pros and cons of my ideas.	
	I proactively identify risk areas to develop practical ideas.	

From the assessment above, identify which part of cognitive confidence you can improve on.

Getting the Logical Thinking Right- Power of Key Stakeholder Questions (KSQ's)

Logical thinking, in itself, is an enormous field. For the moment, I will restrict my thoughts to applying logical thinking for an enhanced executive presence. The good news is that logical thinking is a learnable skill, and by applying a structured process, we can enhance it quite rapidly.

Leaders who are high on executive presence apply a *stakeholder-centric approach* for thinking logically about their ideas. Before they take their ideas to a stakeholder, they ask themselves a very simple question: ***"When I share my idea with the stakeholder, what questions will they need answers to?"*** I like to call these Key Stakeholder Questions (**KSQs**).

Here is a scenario: Suppose you are the CEO of a company and you are about to attend a meeting where a colleague will be sharing a new business idea with you. As you attend the meeting, you will have a list of questions that you want the colleague to answer. Your chances of getting convinced will be directly proportional to the ability of the colleague to answer those questions.

Here are some questions you may have in mind as the CEO:

1. What is the business idea?

2. How is this linked to our strategy?

3. Is there a strong market need for this?

4. What strategy should be used to capture this opportunity?

5. What is the opportunity size?

6. What risks can come our way?

7. Is there a proof of concept?

These 7 questions are the "Key Stakeholder Questions (KSQ's)" i.e. the questions in the mind of the stakeholder.

The good thing is that most of these questions are already organized in a logical manner.

Now, let's say that you are that colleague who will be presenting your idea to the CEO. What happens is, before the meeting, you spend time identifying KSQs?

If you "put yourself in the CEO's place" and ask yourself, "what questions would I need answers to if I were the CEO?", you will be able to identify the KSQs. You can then spend time organizing your presentation accordingly!

Therefore, KSQs can be a very powerful tool for you to look at your ideas/suggestions from a stakeholder's perspective and hence nudge you to apply logical thinking automatically.

Let's go back to Sarah's story.

As you recall, the key issue that Sarah's supervisor felt was that she could not see logic and rationale in what Sarah was recommending. Now, imagine if you are Sarah's supervisor and you know that she has scheduled time with you to propose a new idea, what questions will you need answers to?

As you think through this, you will notice that Sarah's supervisor needs answers to the following questions:

- What is the problem statement?

- Why do we need to solve this problem?

- Is this problem big enough to solve?

- What are the various alternatives to solve this problem?

- Has Sarah objectively considered all these options?

- For the selected option, what risks do we face?

- Can we practically implement the solution proposed?

Sarah's ability to think logically depends on whether or not she has answered these questions. Therefore, one way Sarah can improve her logical thinking is by spending structured time reflecting on these questions.

Two Types of KSQs

In my experience, in most presentations, there are 2 types of KSQ's:

- **Problem Solving KSQs:** These KSQs are relevant when the communicator is trying to propose a solution to a business problem. These problems may include improving operational efficiency, driving productivity, enhancing customer experience, reducing costs, etc.

- **Opportunity Capturing KSQs:** These KSQs are relevant when the communicator is trying to propose an idea to capture more opportunity. These may not be operational problems but new things that the organization can do. These may include developing new products, entering new market segments, white spaces, etc.

While preparing for a presentation, you can apply either or both of these contexts to develop the KSQs that stakeholders may have.

Let's explore this a bit further...

The tables below consist of typical KSQs for both of these scenarios:

Problem Solving KSQs

KSQ	Potential Technique to Answer the Question
What is the problem statement?	Clear definition of the problem statement in 25 words.
Why do we need to solve this problem?	Linkage with the business strategy, or issues with business metrics.
Is this problem big enough to solve?	Data on the impact of not solving the problem
What are the various alternatives to solve this problem?	Laying down at least 2-3 good alternative solutions to solve the problem.
Has Sarah objectively considered all these options?	Showcasing all the options, with pros and cons of each option. Showcasing decision-making criteria followed for idea selection.
For the selected option, what risks do we face?	Plotting and openly sharing risks,
Can we practically implement the solution proposed?	Draft implementation plan with logical timelines.

Opportunity Capturing KSQs

KSQ	Potential Technique to Answer the Question
What is the opportunity?	Clear definition of an opportunity statement in 25 words.
Why do we need to cater to this opportunity?	Linkage with the business strategy,
Is this a big enough opportunity?	Data on the impact of capturing the opportunity.
What are the various alternatives to approach this opportunity?	Laying down at least 2-3 good alternative solution ideas.
Has the person objectively considered all these options?	Showcasing all the options, with pros and cons of each option. Showcasing decision-making criteria followed for idea selection.
For the selected option, what risks do we face?	Plotting and openly sharing risks,
Can we practically implement the solution proposed?	Draft an implementation plan with logical timelines. Sharing pilot approaches or data as needed.

If Sarah had followed a structured (and chronological) approach to identify and answer the KSQs, her ability to influence would have been greatly enhanced.

This is the power of KSQ's! They make us think in a logical manner.

Core issue: Moving from single idea thinking to a business case thinking.

As we reflect on the KSQ's above, we then uncover one of the biggest traps toward logical thinking:

> **"While stakeholders expect that the person giving an idea would have thought through about alternatives, many people are single-idea thinkers."**

When a person who is trying to influence a stakeholder presents a single idea, it raises questions in the mind of the stakeholders on whether the communicator has considered alternatives. If, during the course of the conversation, the listener starts feeling that the person proposing the idea has not considered other alternatives (or dimensions), they may not feel convinced.

Vicious Cycle of Single Idea Thinking

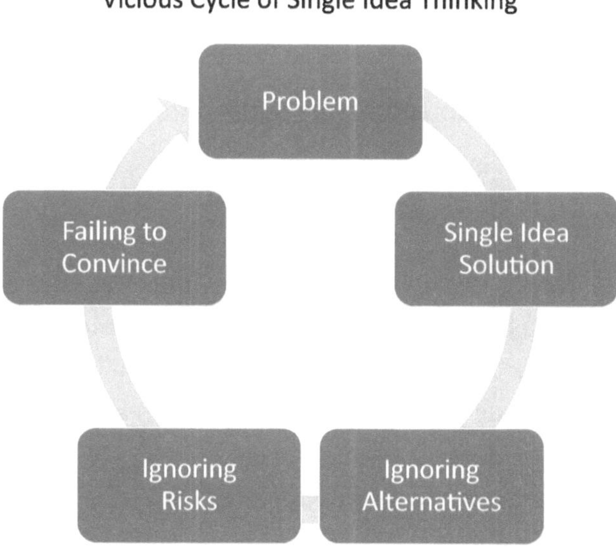

Single idea thinking can put us into a vicious cycle of thinking that a particular problem can only be solved with a single idea. This can lead to not paying attention to other alternatives to solve the problem. When we don't consider other alternatives, we may unconsciously ignore risks of our solution. And, if we haven't explored alternatives or risks in detail, we may find it hard to convince others of our idea.

Leaders with high executive presence have a very different approach toward thinking: **Business Case Thinking**.

Let me first elaborate on the concept of a business case. The question here is, "What is a business case?"

Dictionary definition of a business case is to share justification and cost/benefits for a proposed idea. However, from a very practical standpoint, I feel that a business case is about answering a critical question.

> **"A business case answers a question: What happens if we take action A to solve the problem instead of taking action B?"**

This definition helps us understand that a business case is about:

- Creating multiple options to solve a problem.

- Reflecting on the pros and cons of each solution.

- Selecting and recommending the option after careful consideration.

- Being objective about risks and considering multiple perspectives before making a decision.

Let me highlight an example of this definition in action. A few years ago, I had a chance to observe a presentation by a senior business leader who was trying to influence the top management of his organization to open an office in a new country. Prior to the presentation, the leader had done extensive research on market entry strategies for that country, legalities, talent availability, and opportunities.

At the start of the presentation, the leader covered the market opportunity in great detail. He covered the market size well and was able to also articulate the strategic fit of entering this market for the organization.

What particularly caught my attention, though, were the alternatives.

After having convinced the stakeholders that this country was a good opportunity for the organization, he mentioned that there were "Go-to-market" options for the organization:

- **Option 1:** Establish a direct office and presence.

- **Option 2:** Develop a distributor-led model.

- **Option 3:** Enter into a strategic tie-up.

He covered all 3 options in detail, objectively discussing the pros and cons of each option. He then suggested to the group the option that he would recommend. He explained his proposed option in detail and outlined a phase 1 plan with key "learning measures."

His presentation was fantastic, and he got immediate approval to go ahead with the next steps, along with some guidance. That presentation was a masterclass in business case thinking!

We all left the meeting inspired...

Imagine, what would have happened if in this case the leader would have displayed single-idea thinking? What if the business leader would have only proposed option 1?

Someone from the top management team would have asked the leader if he had considered other alternatives. Someone would have asked him about the risks. If he had displayed single-idea thinking while presenting, chances are that, most likely, he would have been asked to "conduct more research" and present again in the future.

Single idea thinking would not have built enough confidence within the management to give their approval.

As we reflect on the story earlier, let's look at the difference between single-idea thinking and business case thinking through the table below:

Single Idea Thinker	Business Case Thinker
Focuses more on the idea rather than the problem statement.	Focus more on the problem statement, and then on the idea.
Feels that there is only one way to solve the problem.	Thinks about various alternatives to solve the problem, or capitalize on the opportunity.
Tries to sell the idea.	Objectively evaluates all alternatives and selects the best possible.
Has a tendency to fall in love with the idea and, therefore, may not consider the risks enough.	Considers potential risks and communicates them in an authentic manner.

Remember Sarah? Let's look at an example of how Sarah displayed business case thinking while proposing her idea in the next meeting with her supervisor.

"Disheartened but determined, Sarah realized that she needed to enhance her logical thinking skills if she wanted to make a compelling case for her ideas in the future.

She worked with a coach to identify KSQs that her supervisor would have on her idea. As she reflected on the KSQs, Sarah realized that she was specifically unable to answer the following questions in the last meeting:

- Why is this a problem?

- Is this a problem big enough to solve?

- What possible alternative solutions exist to solve the same problem?

Sarah worked in an objective manner to draw the argument that connected her project management proposal with functional strategy. She also compiled data on potential short-term and long-term productivity benefits for the organization.

She then conducted some research by speaking with other organizations on how they were solving similar problem statements. Through this process, she identified 3 different alternatives for solving the problem.

This process honed her ability to structure arguments, anticipate counterarguments, and present compelling, logical frameworks to support her proposal.

Sarah prepared a revised version of her project management proposal. She requested another meeting with her supervisor, who was impressed by her persistence and commitment to growth.

This time, as Sarah presented the refined proposal, she demonstrated a logical and well-supported argument. She confidently explained the rationale behind each step, providing clear evidence of the anticipated benefits, and addressing potential challenges proactively.

She was able to articulate 2-3 different alternative solutions and shared the pros and cons of each alternative. She then covered the alternative she was recommending in detail.

After careful consideration, her supervisor acknowledged the merit of Sarah's proposal. Together, they refined the plan further and agreed to implement the changes, confident in the potential positive impact it would have on the organization.

Here is a discovery:

If we consciously follow the process of identifying KSQs and apply the process of business case thinking, it nudges us to automatically think logically and consider alternatives.

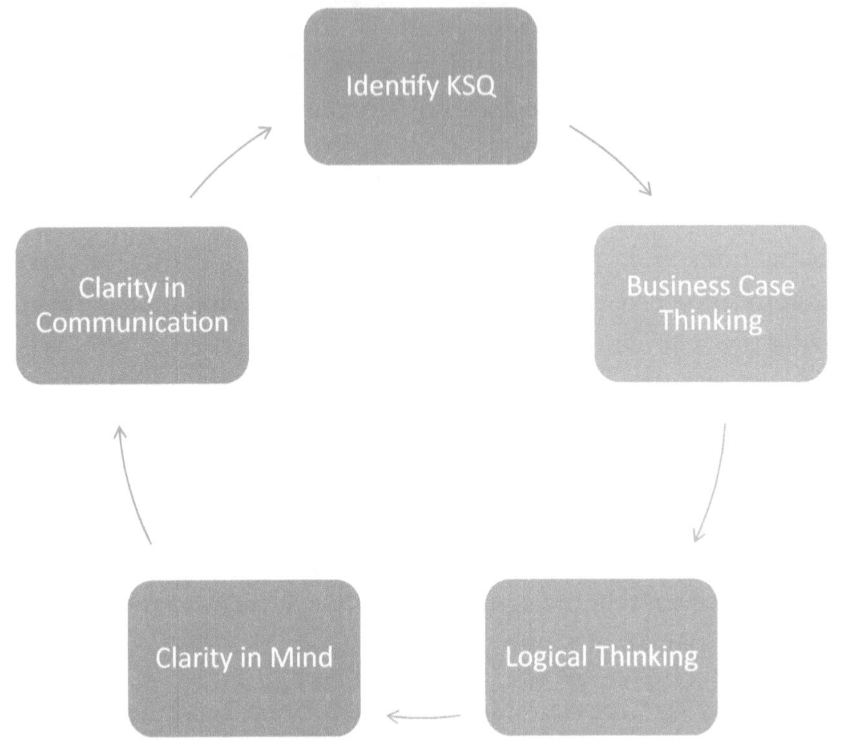

By considering alternatives, our mind starts to think more objectively about the best way to solve problems or capture opportunities. This gives our mind clarity and…

…clarity in mind leads to clarity in communication!

Considering Alternatives: Rule of 3.

One of my friends and colleagues defines strategic thinking in a very unique way. He says that strategic thinking involves coming up with 3 good choices and then choosing from one of those choices to achieve your strategic objective. I have found this framework extremely valuable.

When faced with a problem, the tendency is often to focus on finding a single solution. However, research and practical experience have shown that considering multiple alternatives can lead to more effective problem-solving and decision-making.

Let's see some benefits of the rule of 3:

- **Unleashing Creativity and Innovation:** Generating three good alternatives encourages divergent thinking, unlocking our creative potential. By exploring different possibilities, we expand our perspectives and tap into our imagination. This process stimulates innovation, allowing us to discover unique and unconventional solutions that may have otherwise been overlooked.

- **Overcoming Biases and Assumptions:** Our minds tend to be influenced by biases and preconceived notions, limiting our ability to see beyond the obvious. However, when we challenge ourselves to come up with 3 alternatives, we break free from these mental constraints. This exercise helps us overcome anchoring biases, encouraging us to consider a wider range of options and explore diverse approaches to problem-solving.

- **Enhancing Decision-Making:** Considering three good alternatives empowers us to make more informed decisions. It allows us to evaluate the pros and cons of each option, weighing their strengths and weaknesses. By thoroughly examining multiple alternatives, we can assess the potential risks, benefits, and trade-offs associated with each, leading to more well-rounded and thoughtful decisions.

- **Increasing Problem-Solving Flexibility:** The power of generating three good alternatives lies in the flexibility it provides. It equips us with a range of potential solutions, enabling us to adapt and pivot when circumstances change. Having multiple alternatives at our disposal ensures that we are better prepared to navigate unexpected obstacles and find alternative routes toward resolving the problem at hand.

- **Encouraging Collaboration and Teamwork:** When working in a team, coming up with three good alternatives encourages collaboration and fosters collective problem-solving. Each team member can contribute their unique perspectives, ideas, and suggestions. This collaborative process strengthens teamwork, promotes diversity of thought, and often leads to more comprehensive and innovative solutions.

Therefore, the power of coming out with 3 good alternatives cannot be understated. Another potential benefit of the rule of 3 is that sometimes an ideal solution may be a combination of all 3 alternatives, and this makes our recommendations much more robust.

Here is a story that displays the same:

Rachel was an HR Executive in an organization. For her company, the employee engagement levels were plummeting, leading to decreased productivity and a sense of dissatisfaction among the workforce. As the HR executive responsible for employee well-being, Rachel took it upon herself to find a solution.

Recognizing the importance of considering multiple alternatives, Rachel gathered her team for a brainstorming session. She encouraged them to think beyond the obvious and come up with 3 distinct approaches to address the problem.

The first alternative proposed by the team was to introduce a flexible work arrangement. They believed that by allowing employees to have more control over their work schedules, it would foster a better work-life balance and increase overall job satisfaction. This alternative aimed to empower employees, enhance their engagement, and create a positive work environment.

The second alternative focused on implementing a comprehensive employee recognition program. The team realized that acknowledging and appreciating employees' efforts would significantly impact their motivation and engagement. They suggested designing a system that recognized outstanding performance, celebrated milestones, and provided opportunities for peer-to-peer recognition. This alternative aimed to create a culture of appreciation and instill a sense of pride and accomplishment among employees.

The third alternative involved conducting anonymous employee surveys to gain valuable insights into the underlying issues contributing to the decline in engagement. By understanding the specific pain points and concerns of the workforce, Rachel and her team could develop targeted solutions to address them. This alternative aimed to prioritize employee feedback, foster open communication, and demonstrate the company's commitment to employee well-being.

As Rachel and her team explored these 3 alternatives, they considered the potential benefits, challenges, and implications of each option. They evaluated the feasibility, cost-effectiveness, and expected impact on employee engagement.

Instead of choosing a single approach, Rachel decided to integrate aspects from all 3 alternatives into a comprehensive action plan.

She recognized that a combination of flexible work arrangements, a robust recognition program, and a commitment to listening to employees' voices would yield the best results.

Rachel and her team worked tirelessly to roll out the initiatives, ensuring transparency, providing necessary resources, and continuously monitoring progress.

Over time, the impact of Rachel's approach became evident. Employee engagement levels gradually started to rise, reflected in increased productivity, improved morale, and a stronger sense of camaraderie within the organization. The holistic solution had addressed multiple aspects contributing to the problem, creating a more positive and fulfilling work environment.

Rachel's ability to leverage the power of 3 alternatives had not only solved the initial problem but had also laid the foundation for sustained employee engagement.

Her innovative approach and commitment to finding comprehensive solutions earned her recognition as a valuable asset to the organization.

Putting It Together: IMPACT Framework

As we reflect on all the key principles that we have covered above, there is a one consolidated framework which emerges. I like to call this the IMPACT framework.

IMPACT is a very powerful tool to help you think logically regarding an issue or an idea. By applying this framework, you can rest assured that your presentation has a strong logical connection.

To keep it simple, IMPACT stands for an acronym as well as a chronology. An acronym so that it is easy to remember, and chronology, as it lays down the chronological sequence of thinking as well as that of communication.

Let's understand what IMPACT stands for:

I: Issue or Opportunity

M: Materiality of that issue/opportunity.

P: Power of the issue/opportunity

A: Alternatives to solve the issue, or capitalize on the opportunity.

C: Considerations for decision-making.

T: Tangible plan or next steps.

The purpose of IMPACT is to ensure that, in a structured manner, we are answering all the KSQ's that stakeholders may need answers to. IMPACT also helps us to easily identify potential KSQ's for 2 contexts:

- **Issue resolution context:** This includes situations where we are trying to solve a problem or an issue.

- **Opportunity capture context:** Includes situations in which we are not solving a problem, but trying to capitalise on an opportunity or an innovation.

The table below illustrates typical KSQs in both of these contexts using the IMPACT framework.

KSQ	IMPACT Framework	Issue Resolution Context	Opportunity Capture Context
What is the issue or opportunity?	Issue	Describe the key issue.	Describe the opportunity statement.
Why do we need to cater to this issue/ opportunity?	Materiality	Linkage with the business strategy,	Linkage with the business strategy.
Is this big enough?	Power	Data on the impact of the issue.	Data on the impact of the opportunity
What are the various alternatives we have?	Alternatives	Laying down at least 2-3 good alternative solutions.	Laying down 2-3 alternative ideas.
Has the person objectively considered all these options? For the selected option, what risks do we face?	Considerations & Criteria	Showcasing all the options, with pros and cons of each option. Showcasing decision-making criteria followed for idea selection. Plotting and openly sharing risks,	Showcasing all the options, with pros and cons of each option. Showcasing decision-making criteria followed for idea selection. Plotting and openly sharing risks,
Can we practically implement the solution proposed?	Tangible Plan	Draft an implementation plan with logical timelines. Sharing pilot approaches or data as needed.	Draft an implementation plan with logical timelines. Sharing pilot approaches or data as needed.

By leveraging the IMPACT framework, we are making our minds think in a logical manner. This is also a great way to self-coach ourselves to look at our ideas from other stakeholders' perspective.

Strong ability to think is directly proportional to strong executive presence.

Price Articulation

While tools and techniques like IMPACT can help us to get logical thinking in place, equally critical is precise articulation. During more than 2 decades in my consulting career, I have noticed that several leaders have really smart ideas, but they find them hard to articulate. Particularly, one issue that they struggle with is overtalking!

Let's look at a story on how some of these things play out:

- Anika (name changed) was the CEO of an organization. She was a very competent leader, but she faced one recurring challenge: during strategy meetings, Anika's tendency to over-explain things using long, convoluted sentences left the team confused.

- Despite her achievements, Anika occasionally felt the urge to prove herself to the team. In strategy meetings, this translated into an excessive use of complex explanations and technical jargon to showcase her expertise, inadvertently overwhelming the team.

- Additionally, fearing that her ideas wouldn't be well received, she would over-explain in an attempt to justify and solidify their points, often losing the essence of the message in the process.

- Furthermore, she wanted to showcase a foolproof strategy, and as a result, her sentences were filled with unnecessary information.

- Typically, in these meetings, her team started keeping quiet and did not ask questions. They started fearing that any question will be served with a long answer, which would add to their mental saturation. She found it hard to read these social cues, unaware that her communication style was hindering effective understanding and collaboration.

Anika came out of these strategy meetings frustrated and puzzled as she was not sure where she was going wrong!

Many leaders struggle with articulation, like Anika. Over the years of my practice, I have observed the following reasons why people over-explain.

- **Need for Validation**: People may over-explain to seek validation or approval from others. They believe that by providing excessive details or justifications, they can convince others of their competence or knowledge.

  This behavior is often driven by a fear of being misunderstood or not being taken seriously.

- **Lack of Confidence**: Individuals who lack confidence in their ideas or abilities may resort to over-explaining to compensate for their perceived deficiencies. They may feel the need to provide extensive evidence or explanations to justify their viewpoints, fearing that their ideas may not be accepted, otherwise.

  This also generally happens to those people who have not followed a logical process to arrive at their ideas or recommendations.

- **Desire for Perfection and Detail**: Some individuals have a strong desire for perfection and a strong desire to get into details. They believe that by explaining the idea in great detail, they will be able to create better buy-in.

  However, in this desire for perfection, they may over-explain in an attempt to cover every possible angle. This behavior also happens when the person speaking has not conducted an appropriate "audience analysis."

  They may end up sharing the same amount of detail, irrespective of the listener in front of them.

- **Difficulty Reading Social Cues**: People who struggle with understanding social cues or navigating social situations effectively may over-explain to ensure clarity and avoid potential misunderstandings.

They may not accurately gauge the level of information required or the interest of their audience, leading to excessive explanations.

- **Fear of Rejection or Conflict**: Over-explaining can also stem from a fear of rejection or conflict. Some individuals may anticipate disagreement or pushback and attempt to pre-emptively address any potential objections through thorough explanations.

Self-awareness and humble inquiry are the bridge to precise articulation.

One of the key ways to develop precise articulation is through self-awareness and humble inquiry. Humble inquiry involves asking people for sincere and authentic feedback. It also involves listening to the feedback with an open mind, to deepen your self-awareness.

In the case of Anika, she started realizing that she needed to get some feedback and advice. Therefore, Anika asked for feedback after one such meeting from a colleague who was candid enough to share with her that while facilitating meetings, she had over-explaining tendencies and spoke too much. This colleague also honestly shared the impact this was having on the listeners.

Armed with this feedback, Anika decided to take action. She started a journey of self-reflection, seeking to understand the underlying reasons behind her behavior. With the help of a coach, Anika developed strategies to overcome these challenges.

With support, Anika adopted a simpler and more concise communication style, focusing on conveying her message clearly and effectively. She started:

- Prioritising clarity over excessive detail.

- Crafting concise statements that resonated with the team's understanding.

- Becoming more attuned to the team's reactions, she adjusted her explanations accordingly.

- Actively seeking feedback and encouraged open dialogue, creating an environment where the team felt comfortable asking for clarification when needed..

As a result of this, her strategy meetings became more productive and engaging. The team appreciated the newfound clarity and simplicity in their communication, allowing for greater collaboration and alignment.

As evident in this story, self-awareness and reflection are the bridge to precise articulation. Therefore, in order to achieve precise articulation, we must investigate if there are any underlying insecurities that are the cause.

To discover these, I suggest taking a very small self-assessment on the next page.

Self-Assessment

Instructions: Rate yourself on a scale of 1 to 5 for each of the factors above. Choose the rating that best reflects your typical behavior and tendencies. For each factor, the rating scale is as follows:

1: Rarely exhibit the behavior.

2: Occasionally exhibit the behavior,

3: Sometimes exhibit the behavior.

4: Often exhibit the behavior.

5: Frequently exhibit the behavior.

Factors	1 - Rarely	2 - Occasionally	3 - Sometimes	4 - Often	5 - Frequently
Need for validation	Rarely seeks validation or approval	Occasionally seeks validation	Sometimes seeks validation	Often seeks validation	Frequently seeks validation
Insecurity or Lack of Confidence	Rarely insecure or Lack Confidence	Occasionally insecure	Sometimes insecure	Often insecure	Frequently insecure
Desire for Perfection	Rarely desires perfection	Occasionally desires perfection	Sometimes desires perfection	Often desires perfection	Frequently desires perfection
Difficulty Reading Social Cues	Rarely struggles with social cues	Occasionally struggles	Sometimes struggles	Often struggles	Frequently struggles
Fear of Rejection or conflict	Rarely fears rejection or conflict	Occasionally Fears	Sometimes fears	Often fears	Frequently fears

Remember, this self-assessment is meant to provide self-reflection and awareness.

It can serve as a starting point for personal growth and development in effective executive presence.

Using Precise Language

Precise language in presentations is crucial for conveying information clearly and effectively. Precision helps to eliminate ambiguity and ensures that the audience understands your message accurately.

Here are some tips on how to use precise language:

- **Make language specific**: Sometimes, people who don't have precise articulation use vague sentences (or generic language) to describe something. Therefore, the listener may not understand what they are trying to say. As much as possible, try to use language that is very specific. Here is an example-

  - **Non-precise:** "Our numbers are not good, and we need to improve our sales."

  - **Precise:** "We need to increase our sales by 10% in the next quarter."

- **Be specific with numbers and data**: Data is a fact, and it is real. People who don't have precise articulation may end up using adjectives to describe the data. Precise articulators follow a simple method; they just share the actual numbers!

  - **Non-precise:** "We had a significant increase in customer satisfaction."

  - **Precise:** "Our customer satisfaction rating improved from 75% to 80% in the past year."

- **Power of numbering**: Another technique that can enhance articulation is the power of numbering. Let's take an example, suppose you are giving an update on a project which is behind schedule. Here is how this can be covered:

  - **Non-precise:** "The project is running late because of multiple issues and challenges. We have some resource constraints that are blocking us. Also, the scope of the project is always increasing, and there is a lot of confusion in the team."

- ○ **Precise:** "The project encountered three major challenges: resource constraints, communication gaps, and scope creep."

- **Keep the sentence structure small:** If possible, while presenting, keep the sentence structure short. People who are not precise tend to use very long sentence structures.

  - ○ **Non-precise:** "With regards to the forthcoming marketing campaign, which we have been working on for the past few months, I wanted to bring to your attention that, based on our extensive research and analysis of consumer behavior and market trends, we have come to the conclusion that, in order to effectively reach our target audience and maximize our brand visibility, it would be highly beneficial for us to leverage social media platforms such as Facebook, Instagram, and Twitter, as well as other digital marketing channels including email marketing and search engine optimization."

  - ○ **Precise:** "For our upcoming marketing campaign, our research shows that utilising social media platforms, along with digital marketing channels like email and SEO, will optimise our brand visibility among the target audience."

Don't combine multiple, divergent thoughts while talking about one topic.

One of the key issues that non-precise speakers face is that, while talking about one topic, they will quickly jump to another (and another), making the listener utterly confused.

This typically happens when the speaker has not really thought through their own main messages and has a high need to be listened to.

Here is an example: "I want to bring up an issue regarding leveraging data. While we understand that data is good for decision-making, the data being put in the CRM is not accurate, and there are too many systems to manage the data.

In fact, now the data is maintained in Excel as well as in the CRM. I also feel that by leveraging too much data, we are making people operate only like executors, and there is a lot of demotivation in the team!"

As we understand, listening to something like this can be exhausting for listeners and can leave them completely confused! Moreover, it impacts the credibility of the speaker.

In this case, it is critical for the speaker to take 1-2 specific issues that they would like to bring up!

Time yourself!

One good practice that works specifically for presentations is to go through all the main messages by timing yourself. For example, if you are about to make a presentation covering 8-10 key points and messages, and you have only 45 minutes to cover them all, you can do a dry run and time yourself to see how much time it actually takes.

This will help you to check if there are some areas where you need to reduce time, or whether you need to reduce or combine some messages.

Summary:

- Cognitive confidence is the individual's ability to build confidence with others by showcasing logical thinking and by communicating with clarity..

- **Cognitive confidence depends on two key attributes:**

  o Logical Thinking.

  o Precise Articulation.

- Key stakeholder questions can be a very powerful tool for you to look at your ideas/suggestions from a stakeholder's perspective and hence nudge you to apply logical thinking automatically.

- IMPACT is a powerful framework to convert the KSQs to a logical thinking framework. IMPACT stands for:

  o I: Issue or Opportunity

  o M: Materiality of that issue/opportunity.

  o P: Power of the issue/opportunity

  o A: Alternatives to solve the issue, or capitalize on the opportunity.

  o C: Considerations for decision-making

  o T: Tangible plan or next steps.

- Self-awareness is a bridge for precise articulation. People who are not precise articulators can display:

  o Need for validation.

  o Desire for perfection.

  o Lack of confidence.

  o Difficulty in reading social cues.

  o Fear of rejection.

- Try to use precise language when communicating. Some tips include:

  - Make language-specific.

  - Use actual numbers wherever possible.

  - Leverage the power of numbering.

  - Keep sentence structures small.

  - Don't combine multiple divergent points.

  - Time yourself.

Part 3

Evoking Emotions Through Communication

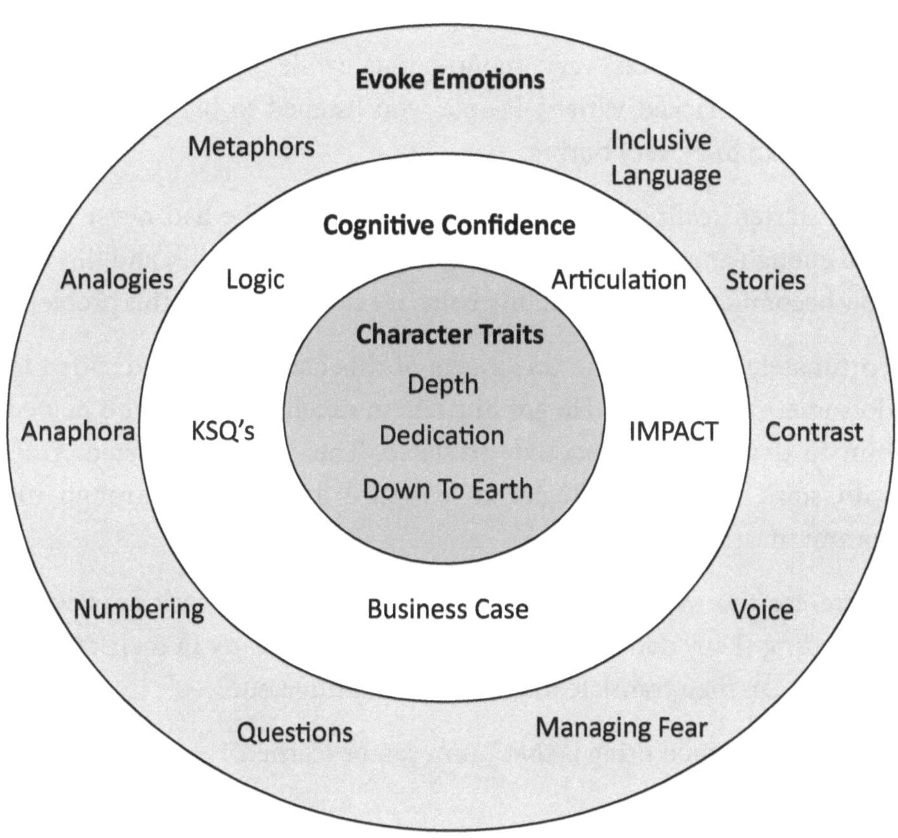

Evoking Emotions For Aura

Amit was a business executive in a large organization. He had risen through his dedication and hard work within the ranks of the organization and was now heading a small business unit within the company.

However, he was now facing a peculiar problem. He was not perceived as an inspiring leader within the organization. One of the key contributors to this was Amit's lack of executive presence. Though, while making business presentations, Amit had some logically constructed ideas, his ability to present was not very good.

Frequently during his presentations, he used a lot of non-words (like aa…). His voice was very monotonous while presenting, and his presentations lacked variety. People who listened to his presentations found them to be very boring.

Amit started realizing that throughout his career, he had never really paid enough attention to sharpening his presentation skills, and this was now becoming a major capability issue. He needed to solve this problem.

Fortunately, for Amit, he was aware of this challenge and decided to do something about it. He got himself an excellent coach who helped him to develop his executive presence. The coach supported Amit with some pointed strategies to enhance engagement through his communication.

There are too many business leaders like Amit who lack aura while presenting. They don't pay attention to this "skill" early in their careers, and this can then translate into a career-limiting issue.

However, the good thing is that "Aura can be learned"!

It is true that some people have an aura naturally, just as some people have natural strategic thinking abilities. However, just as strategic thinking can be learned and developed, so can an aura!

It just requires patience, focus, and practice.

Aura can be developed by incorporating some very specific techniques in our communication. During the course of my work, I have observed that leaders who are able to evoke emotions intentionally leverage 10 presentation techniques.

I like to refer to them as the "super 10" techniques. These are super because they can be learned in a fast manner and create an immediate impact.

Let's look at what these techniques are!

Technique 1: Metaphors

A few years ago, I was interacting with a business leader who was heading a large sales organization. This sales organization operated through distributors, and therefore, it was critical for them to ensure that each distributor invests in the business to offer a consistent customer experience.

During a meeting, he was trying to communicate to his team the power of following a consistent process to manage large distributors. He wanted everyone in the team to understand what an ideal distributor would look like and how following a structured process can help them to create such ideal channel partners.

As he was thinking about how to communicate this message, I encouraged him to consider using metaphor as a technique. We discussed what possible metaphors he could leverage.

After some thought, he finalized the word "lighthouse"! He realized that an ideal distributor is like a lighthouse for the company and other distributors because they inspire others to achieve the same standards of excellence.

Therefore, during his presentation, he started by sharing the concept of a lighthouse and how it gives a directional sense to everyone. He then mentioned to the team an example of one distributor who was already a lighthouse and the journey that was undertaken to make that distributor achieve the underlying standards.

He then communicated with the team that their shared mission is to create more such lighthouse distributors by being lighthouse creators.

As you can imagine, this was a very inspirational and energizing message for the audience! The metaphor of the lighthouse really worked!

As evident in the story above, a metaphor is a figure of speech in which a word or phrase is applied to an object or action. It is a way of describing something or someone by showing their similarity with something else.

We all use metaphors several times during our personal life. Here are some examples of metaphors that we generally use:

- He has a heart of gold.

- It's raining cats and dogs.

- You are a breath of fresh air!

Metaphors add color to our communication and make us communicate in an impactful manner.

Metaphors also ensure that the listener has understood and becomes emotionally involved in the conversation.

People with strong executive presence **deliberately use metaphors** in their communication. This is because they realize the power of metaphors in communicating their message.

One major advantage of using metaphors is that they stick in people's minds. And when a message sticks, it has been well communicated. This also creates a common language within the team and common reference points!

For example, in the above story, when goals were set by each individual, there were goals like, "How many lighthouse partners will I create?" When the reviews were done, the questions they were answering included:

- How many lighthouses have we created?

- How do we adapt our lighthouse creation process?

- How do we leverage existing lighthouses to influence other partners?

Super powerful!

Let's look at some more examples of metaphors that can be used while communicating in the business world.

- **Statement:** We have a large customer base, with many customers contributing very small amounts, and therefore we are unable to focus on large customers.

  ○ Alternative with Metaphor: We have a long tail of customers, and we need to cut the long tail.

- **Statement:** We need to add more senior talent and resources in this business.

  ○ Alternative with Metaphor: We need to add more talent firepower in this business.

Obviously, when using metaphors, it is advisable to use some criteria. Here are some points to keep in mind:

1. **Relevance:** Is the metaphor I am planning to use relevant in this situation?

2. **Stickiness:** Is this metaphor powerful enough for people to remember?

3. **Simplicity:** Can the metaphor communicate the message in a simple manner?

Leveraging Visual Metaphors:

A few years ago, we were working with a client to develop a module on conducting career conversations for managers. While developing the content of this module, we started thinking about the challenges that managers face while engaging in career conversations with their team members.

We realized that most managers faced challenges in dealing with ambiguity while conducting these conversations. There can be ambiguity on a team member's career aspiration, their own understanding of their strengths, and even ambiguity around career options available to the individual.

To summarize, we realized that to conduct effective career conversations, managers should be comfortable with ambiguity and adopt an "exploration mindset." This would also ensure that they start enjoying these conversations.

As we were thinking about the above, we asked ourselves, "What metaphor can we use for this message?" As the client and we brainstormed, one of the colleagues suggested the metaphor of trekking. He mentioned that when we go on a trek, we are clear about the goal (the end point of the trek) but we are unclear about the final path we will take. This is because while conducting a trek, we may encounter different situations including weather, obstacles on the way, etc. Therefore, a professional trekker carries a bag with tools. These tools can be utilized to navigate the trek if needed.

He mentioned that career conversations are similar. It's like the manager and the employee are going on a joint trek, and as the conversation unfolds, the manager should leverage the right tools.

As expected, we all were able to instantly connect with this idea. We, therefore, put a visual representation of the trek in our program content. This included some relevant images. We then linked those visual representations with career conversations.

This technique worked brilliantly for us, as managers could easily draw the correlation and understand the right mindset that they needed to display while conducting career conversations.

Visual metaphors can be a powerful tool to convey complex ideas in a memorable way. In visual metaphors, we use images or diagrams to describe the issue or the solution. Visual metaphors ensure that listeners find our content more relatable. There are higher chances that they will remember what we have covered because images stick!

Here are some tips on leveraging visual metaphors:

- Very clearly identify the core message that you want to deliver. In the example I shared, the core message was around being comfortable with the ambiguous nature of career conversations.

- Select the relevant metaphor. Think about various metaphor examples you can give. Develop many options, but select the metaphor which is relevant and relatable to your audience.

- Decide the right time in your presentation to leverage the visual metaphor.

- Put the relevant images of visual metaphor into your presentation. Try to avoid putting too many images. One to 2 powerful images are good enough.

- Be clear about the script you will use when introducing the metaphor. The words you use can go a long way to make a lasting impact.

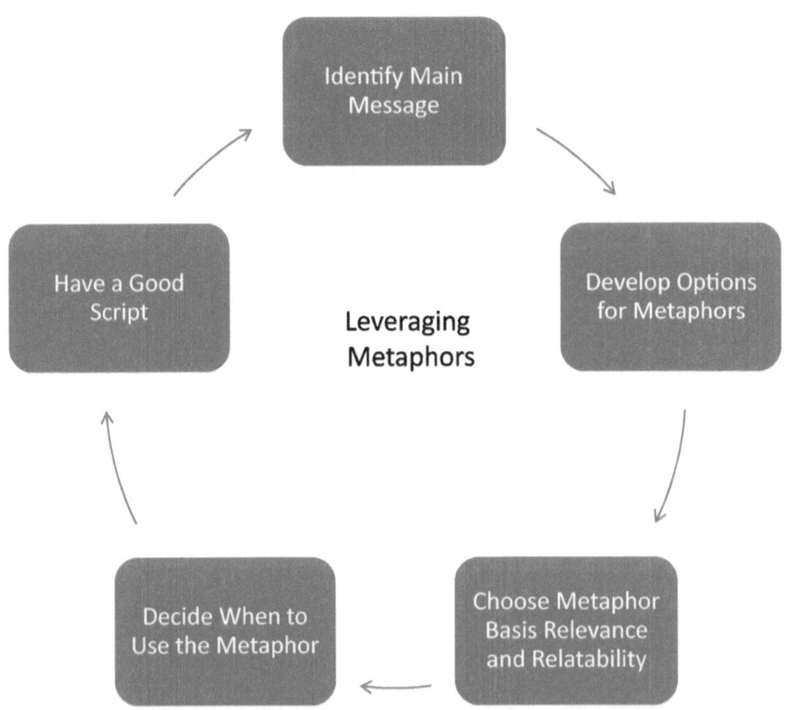

Technique 2: Analogies

Analogy is a comparison between one thing and another, typically for the purpose of explanation or clarification. Unlike a metaphor, the point of an analogy is not merely to *show*, but also to *explain*. Therefore, an analogy follows an explanation on why you are making a comparison, so that people can understand.

One of the most quoted examples of analogy is from William Shakespeare's "As You Like It." Here it is:

> "All the world's a stage, and all the men and women merely players. They have their exits and their entrances, and one man in his time plays many parts. His acts being 7 ages."

One of the best demonstrations of analogies in the business world is in Simon Sinek's inspiring TED talk on "How Great Leaders Inspire Action."

Simon Sinek often uses powerful analogies to convey his ideas and insights. For example, in this TED Talk, he introduces the concept of "The Golden Circle," where he compares successful leaders and organizations to a target with 3 concentric circles.

"What,"

(outer circle),

"How" (middle circle),

and "Why" (inner circle).

He uses this to explain that great leaders start with "Why" – their purpose and beliefs – before delving into "How" they do things and "What" they offer.

Here is another well-known example of an analogy:

Dr. A.P.J. Abdul Kalam, the former President of India and a highly respected scientist, often used analogies to inspire and motivate people. One of his famous analogies is comparing dreams to wings:

"Dreams are not those which come while we are sleeping. Dreams are those which do not let you sleep."

In this analogy, Dr. Kalam compares dreams to wings, suggesting that true dreams are not passive or fleeting thoughts that occur during sleep, but rather aspirations and goals that drive a person to take action and work tirelessly toward achieving them. Just as wings help a bird soar and achieve great heights, dreams provide the motivation and direction needed to reach one's full potential.

This analogy reflects Dr. Kalam's belief in the power of dreams and the importance of nurturing ambitious visions that lead to meaningful actions.

He often encouraged young people to dream big and work hard to turn those dreams into reality, highlighting the idea that dreams can be transformative and lead to significant achievements.

Dr. A.P.J. Abdul Kalam's analogies continue to resonate with people in India and beyond, inspiring them to pursue their goals with passion and determination. His ability to use simple yet impactful analogies is one of the reasons why he remains an admired and revered figure in India's history.

When using an analogy to express your point of view, it's useful to keep the following guidelines in mind:

1. While selecting the analogy, make sure that you are using analogies which are <u>familiar to the listeners</u>. Comparisons to well-known objects, stories, and images are better because then the listeners can immediately connect with them.

2. Select an analogy in which there are <u>many similarities between the points you are trying to compare</u>. This ensures that listeners can understand the message without confusion.

3. Avoid using analogies that make people feel that the road ahead is very complicated (unless you want them to feel that way). This is because when we give an analogy of something considered difficult, it can reduce the team's energy to solve it. Here are some examples of these:

   a. Working on this project is like climbing Mount Everest!

   b. Implementing this new strategy is like performing brain surgery!

   c. This project is like a cart with square wheels; it is going nowhere!

One of the core objectives of analogies is to inspire action! As leaders, we want to raise team energy and not deplete team energy.

Therefore, selecting the right analogy, even in trying circumstances, can inspire positive energy.

Here is an example of this:

The Sales Director of a company wanted to inspire his team and motivate them for a challenging quarter. The Sales Director used the analogy of a sports team preparing for a championship game:

> *"Team, we're gearing up for a crucial quarter ahead, and I want you to think of our strategy as preparing for a championship game. We are the athletes, training hard to achieve peak performance."*

Just like athletes study their opponents, we'll analyse our competitors to identify their weaknesses and capitalize on our strengths. Our leads and prospects are like the fans cheering for us; let's engage with them and turn them into loyal customers.

The sales pipeline is our playing field, and we must navigate it strategically to score big wins.

Remember, every member of this team plays a crucial role in winning the championship, and I have complete confidence that, together, we will bring home the trophy."

In this analogy, the Sales Director drew parallels between the sales team's efforts and the preparation of a sports team for a championship game.

By doing so, the Sales Director motivated the sales team and encouraged them to approach their sales activities with the determination needed to achieve success.

The three-step process for sharing analogies:

As we reflect on the story of the Sales Director, we can identify a very simple 3-step process for sharing analogies. These 3 steps are:

1. Tell,

2. Explain

3. Leverage

Step 1: Tell

As simple as it sounds, step 1 is just telling the listeners the analogy. Here is how the Sales Director did this:

"Team, we're gearing up for a crucial quarter ahead, and I want you to think of our strategy as preparing for a championship game. We are the athletes, training hard to achieve peak performance."

Step 2: Explain

After telling the analogy, explain how the analogy is linked to the topic. Here is how the Sales Director did this:

"Just like athletes study their opponents, we'll analyse our competitors to identify their weaknesses and capitalize on our strengths. Our leads and prospects are like the fans cheering for us; let's engage with them and turn them into loyal customers."

Step 3: Leverage

This step involves leveraging the analogy to evoke emotions in listeners. You want the analogy to "raise energy." Here is how the Sales Director did this:

"The sales pipeline is our playing field, and we must navigate it strategically to score big wins. Remember, every member of this team plays a crucial role in winning the championship, and I have complete confidence that, together, we will bring home the trophy."

So, next time, when you are planning to use an analogy, think about the 3-step process of "Tell, Explain, Leverage."

Practice Exercise

Think about an upcoming presentation that you have. Identify the core message you want to leave your listeners with and identify an analogy you can give.

____

____

____

____

____

____

Tell: Write down below the words you will use to tell them of the analogy.

____

____

____

____

____

____

Explain: Now, write down how you will plan the analogy to your audience by drawing at least 2 parallels:

____

____

____

____

____

____

____

Leverage: Write down below the words you will use to leverage the analogy to evoke positive emotions.

____

____

____

____

____

____

Technique 3: Anaphora

Anaphora is a rhetorical device used in writing and speaking where a word or phrase is repeated at the beginning of successive sentences, clauses, or phrases. It is a powerful technique that adds emphasis, rhythm, and emotional impact to the message.

Anaphora is commonly used in inspiring speeches and persuasive writing to create a memorable and persuasive effect.

Let's take an example of anaphora:

"Every day, every hour, every minute, we strive to be better. Every challenge, every setback, every obstacle, we face with determination. Every success, every achievement, every milestone, we celebrate with pride."

As we notice above, the word "every" is repeated at the beginning of each sentence.

This repetition creates a sense of consistency, reinforces the message, and makes the sentences more impactful, leaving a lasting impression on the audience.

Anaphora serves the purpose of delivering the message in an inspirational manner. People who are experts in using anaphora use it very frequently, and sometimes the audience does not even realize that anaphora is being used… they just get inspired!

One of the most well-known examples of anaphora is Barack Obama's inauguration speech in 2009. Here is an example of how he used anaphora in his inspiring speech. In this example, "Our" is anaphora:

"Our nation is at war against a far-reaching network of violence and hatred. Our economy is badly weakened, a consequence of greed and irresponsibility on the part of some, but also our collective failure to make hard choices and prepare the nation for a new age. Homes have been lost, jobs shed, businesses shuttered. Our health care is too costly, our schools fail too many, and each day brings further evidence that the ways we use energy strengthen our adversaries and threaten our planet."

This particular speech by Obama has been considered one of the most inspiring speeches. He has used anaphora many times in this speech.

While the above example is from the political leadership field, Anaphora are also used for inspirational communicators in the corporate world.

One example of this is Satya Nadella. When Satya Nadella became the CEO of Microsoft, he sent the widely published first email as the CEO. Here are some of his messages from that email where anaphora is used:

Excerpt One

"I am here for the same reason I think most people join Microsoft — to change the world through technology that empowers people to do amazing things. I know it can sound hyperbolic, and yet it's true. We have **done it**, we're **doing it** today, and we are the team that will **do it again**.",

Excerpt Two

We are the only ones who can harness the power of software and deliver it through devices and services that truly empower every individual and every organization. **We are the only** company with a history and continued focus on building platforms and ecosystems that create broad opportunity.

So inspiring these messages are, and we can visualize the power of anaphora through these!

Here are some practical tips to help you effectively use anaphora:

- **Identify the key idea or theme**: Determine the main message you want the anaphora to convey. One way of doing that is to identify one specific emotion that you want the listeners to feel. Typically, a wonderful message to drive through anaphora is the power of collective working.

- **Choose a repeating word or phrase**: select a word or phrase that aligns with your key idea. The repeated word should be strong, meaningful, and relevant to your message. The repeated word does not have to be very complex and can be words that we use in regular communication.

- **Use parallel sentence structures**: Craft sentences that follow a similar structure, making it easy for the audience to recognize the repetition. Try to keep the length of sentences in which you are using anaphora similar; this creates a strong rhythm and impact.

- **Start sentences with the repeated word or phrase**: Place the chosen word or phrase at the beginning of each sentence, clause, or phrase where you want the anaphora to occur. This placement highlights the repetition and reinforces the message.

- **Avoid overuse**: While anaphora can be powerful, using them excessively can diminish their impact. Use anaphora strategically and sparingly, focusing on key points where repetition will have the most significant effect.

- **Practice reading aloud:** Read your writing or speech aloud to see how the anaphora flows and impacts the rhythm and cadence. Make adjustments, as needed, to enhance the overall effect.

As a leader, you can use anaphora to do the following:

1. **To create emphasis:** When we repeatedly use the same word (or sentence structure), we are able, as communicators, to put emphasis on key points that we want our listeners to take. These repeated cycles of emphasis ensure that our messages stick.

2. **To inspire:** Anaphora is a very powerful communication device to inspire people and evoke positive emotions. It builds energy in the listeners and inspires them to act.

3. **To add variety:** Anaphora also helps us to build variety in our presentation. It helps to keep the audience engaged and tuned into our presentations.

Technique 4: Numbering

Numbers have a unique ability to capture attention, provide structure, and make information more memorable. When used strategically, numbering can transform ordinary communication into impactful and persuasive messages that resonate with the audience.

There are numerous advantages of using numbering as a technique; let's take an example.

Suppose you are attending a business presentation on actions that the team needs to understand to drive growth. The presenter mentions the phrase, "There are 3 things we need to do to drive growth." What is the impact of these words on you as a listener?

The moment we hear these words, it engages our senses and has the following benefits:

- **They generate curiosity:** Now, we need to find out what those 3 things are!

- **They generate stickiness:** If the points make logical sense, these three points will stick.

- **They generate trust:** You feel that the presenter has done needed research and is now sharing something which is credible and trustworthy.

- **They generate a feeling of priority:** Anytime we hear phrases like "we need to do 3 things," they automatically generate an inherent sense of importance, which often needs prioritisation.

Here is an example of how I saw this transpire in real life:

The CEO of a large organization was trying to drive a strategic roadmap to promote innovation within the organization. To inspire and engage the team around this, the CEO organized a forum of 60 key leaders of the organization.

His objective was that, through this forum, the team should be able to identify innovation possibilities for the organization.

The CEO started with a very inspirational presentation on how innovation was deeply seeded within the organization's DNA. He took the team through past innovations of the organization and how these innovations were the reason for the tremendous growth of the organization.

The CEO then mentioned that, in order to drive innovation 2.0 within the organization, the leadership needed to do three things:

1. **Turbo-charge growth:** This meant developing new innovations on white spaces to create new markets for the organisation.

2. **Raise the profitability:** This meant developing new innovations to increase profitability and drive better efficiency.

3. **Embed innovation into the organisation culture:** This included creating a high-energy organisation where everyone contributes to innovation.

These three things stood out clearly to everyone in the team and aligned everyone toward the purpose.

Later in the meeting, teams worked in small groups to develop short-term, mid-term, and long-term innovation projects under each theme!

They all put together a long list of possible projects for innovation and left the forum charged with the new innovation mission in hand.

As you consider using this technique, here are some helpful tips to consider:

Create a Clear Outline:

Before you start crafting your presentation, outline the key points you want to cover, and organize them in a logical sequence.

Number each main point to create a clear structure that guides your audience through the presentation.

Use Numerical Sequences:

Incorporate numbered lists or steps to present information in a sequential and easy-to-follow manner.

For example, "5 Key Strategies for Success" or "3 Steps to Improve Productivity."

Prioritize Key Messages:

Numbering helps to convey priority and importance. Place your most critical points at the beginning of the presentation.

Keep it Concise:

Use numbering to make your content more concise and to the point. Avoid lengthy explanations under each point; instead, provide brief and clear statements that communicate the main idea concisely.

Be Consistent:

Stick to a consistent numbering style throughout your presentation.

Rule of Three: If possible, follow the golden rule of 3. That means to share a list of 3 items if possible. The Rule of Three is a powerful rhetorical device that has been used for centuries in communication, writing, and storytelling.

It suggests that ideas or concepts presented in groups of 3 are more memorable, engaging, and persuasive to audiences.

The human brain naturally gravitates toward patterns and threes, making it an effective technique to enhance communication and leave a lasting impact on listeners or readers.

Create Visual Impact:

Incorporate numbered slides with visually appealing designs to reinforce your message.

Use colors, fonts, and layout to make the numbering stand out and catch the audience's eye.

Summarize with Numbering:

In your conclusion, use numbered lists to summarize the main points and reinforce the key messages you want your audience to remember.

By effectively using the power of numbering in your presentations, you can enhance the structure, clarity, and impact of your content, leaving a lasting impression on your audience.

Practice Exercise

Think about an upcoming presentation that you have. Identify the core message you want to leave your listeners with, and think about how you can use numbering as a technique:

____

____

____

____

Use the rule of 3 to identify 3 key actions you want the audience to take away:

____

____

____

____

Identify in what ways you will leverage the power of numbering during and after the presentation:

____

____

____

____

Technique 5: Questions with Strategic Pauses

At the 2019 Women in the World Summit, Indra Nooyi spoke about "Truths from the top." This was one of Indra Nooyi's most inspiring conversations about the lessons she learned while being CEO of PepsiCo.

At the start of this conversation, Indra Nooyi spoke about how the senior leadership of PepsiCo was trying to build an organization with purpose.

While talking about this, Indra Nooyi framed the 4 questions that they were answering:

1. What could PepsiCo do for society beyond financial returns?

2. How do we balance our portfolio with fun products and products that are better and good for customers?

3. How do we make a company that does right by the environment?

4. How do we allow our employees to bring their whole selves to work?

These 4 questions at the start of the conversation created an immediate impact on the listeners and hooked them into an exciting conversation.

Using rhetorical questions can have a profound impact on how messages are received and understood. Rhetorical questions don't demand answers, but prompt the audience to think, reflect, and engage with the content in a deeper and more personal way.

Rhetorical questions serve as powerful attention-grabbers, as they immediately capture an audience's focus. This engagement is especially valuable in presentations and conversations, where the goal is to make a lasting impression.

By presenting the information in the form of a question, we are able to engage the audience in a journey of discovery. They create curiosity and increase the chances of retention of the message.

More importantly, using questions while presenting also forms a connection between the presenter and the listener, as they discover the answers to the question together.

Let's look at another example of this.

Amrita was a middle management business leader in a large financial services organization. Her supervisor had assigned her an innovation business project. In this project, she had to conduct a pilot roll-out of a new business line for a year, and after that, she had to make a presentation to the management on how the organization should scale the business.

Amrita thought hard about this presentation at the end of the year and put together a strong business case document with clear recommendations. However, she also realized that to get approvals on her ideas, she would need to present them in an engaging manner.

As Amrita started her presentation, she mentioned to the group, "I am sure all of you are very keen to look at the results of our pilot and see what the next steps should be. I am sure you have several questions in your mind, including:

- Why did we start this pilot and its linkage to our strategy?

- What assumptions did we make while planning, and were we able to validate those assumptions during execution?

- What learnings did we derive, and how did we adapt the idea?

- Is there a business case to scale this idea, and if yes, how do we go about it?

She then mentioned that her presentation flow revolves around these questions, and she will ensure she is able to adequately cover the responses.

This start hooked the management team into her presentation immediately and raised the level of excitement within the group.

Amrita went on to deliver a great presentation!

Here are some key do's and don'ts to keep in mind while developing these questions:

Dos:

- **Keep in mind your audience:** Amrita did a great job in understanding the seniority of her audience and ensured that rhetorical questions were "at their level." The same questions may not have worked for a different audience.

- **Keep them concise:** Rhetorical questions are supposed to be simple and concise. Our objective is to make them stick!

- **Tie them with your presentation:** Amrita did a great job in ensuring that her presentation covered the rhetorical questions. It is critical that the questions are related to the main messages you want to communicate.

- **Strategically place them:** Insert questions at critical instances, either at the start, middle, or the end of the communication.

- **Use silence:** Rhetorical questions as a technique work if there is a short 2-3 seconds gap between each question. It's not a great strategy to not give a gap at all as that won't let the audience internalize the questions. Too long gaps are also avoidable as that can confuse the listeners.

Don'ts:

- **Avoid overdoing them:** While rhetorical questions are great, they lose impact if we use them too frequently in a presentation. Ideally, 1-2 insertions are good enough.

- **Watch your tone:** When sharing questions, it is critical to avoid a tone that patronizes the audience. It is recommended to use a "learning tone" as much as possible.

- **Avoid predictable questions:** Avoid stating questions that have predictable responses. Those types of questions do not create engagement.

- **Don't speak too fast:** Speaking too fast while sharing questions beats the purpose of using this technique. We want people to be in a reflective mood, so use a moderate pace of speech.

Questions make an impact with strategic pauses:

Questions on their own do create an impact; however, this impact gets multiplied if questions are followed by strategic pauses.

A strategic pause is a brief pause after asking a question. These are not long or empty pauses, but little breaks that create impact. Typically, these pauses are not more than 1-2 seconds. In some cases, we can also have a 3-second pause, but that's used more when you want to create a bit of a dramatic effect.

Pauses help the people who are listening to us to process information and stay engaged in the conversation. They also help us to break the monotony of the presentation. Pauses also give a feeling to the listeners that the person communicating is confident and in control.

Pauses also help you to lay emphasis on the key points of your presentation. Additionally, they keep our sentences short, so that our articulation is precise.

Furthermore, in case you have a tendency to forget, pauses can also help you to structure your mind and prepare for the next point!

When using pauses, here are some tips to follow:

Plan your pauses in advance.

While working on a presentation, decide in advance after which points or questions you will take a pause. Remember, a lot of people who come across as natural presenters are actually well-prepared presenters.

Use pause time as an eye contact time.

Think about a time when you were presenting to an audience and you made the mistake of giving eye contact to only a few people. Many of us would have faced this situation, and we later regret the fact that we missed connecting with a few individuals.

Pauses can serve as a good tool to solve this problem. Decide in advance that you will use pauses as eye contact time. Therefore, while taking pauses, deliberately give eye contact to stakeholders that you may have inadvertently missed.

Think about your pauses as punctuation.

When we speak, the audience is not able to see punctuation marks (commas, full stops, etc). While identifying where to pause, think about them as virtual punctuation marks. Use short pauses for a comma and slightly longer pauses when finishing a sentence.

Practice Time!

Look at the text below. Imagine that you are about to speak this. Identify areas where you can take a pause. (Deliberately, punctuation has been removed from this text).

"Thanks everyone for your time. I am happy to share with you today an update on our recent digital service app. While creating this app, we were trying to answer a few questions: number one, what parts of our service experience can be self-serviced; number 2, how do we make the user experience and navigation simple; and number 3, how do we motivate customers to start using this application."

How did that go for you? I am sure, through this very simple example, it's clear to you when and how to use pauses!

Technique 6: Inclusive Language

Making people feel included is a very important part of executive presence. Feeling included literally means "feeling part of." When we, as listeners, hear someone and we feel included, we feel more connected to them.

When we feel more connected to a speaker, there are higher chances that we will be more engaged in the conversation, and we will participate in their success. Alternatively, if we feel excluded in a meeting, there are high chances that we will be disengaged.

Think about the last time when you were hearing someone and you felt excluded. What did the person do to make you feel that way? What was the impact of this on your motivation to support this individual?

Inclusion is a big area, and therefore, for our current objective, I would focus on a very critical component of inclusion - "inclusive language."

All of us naturally have a language of speaking. Our choice of words, the way we speak, comes from the way we are naturally. There are some people who naturally speak in an inclusive manner. These individuals take other people along when they speak and make them feel more connected. However, several people may generally speak in a non-inclusive manner.

Therefore, one of the most critical issues to watch out for is how much, as a speaker, you have a tendency to use non-inclusive language.

This is a bit hard to catch, as many people may not be self-aware enough to identify that they struggle with this issue.

Let's look at Alex's story:

Alex was a seasoned business leader known for his expertise in marketing strategies. He was invited to present at a prestigious industry conference where he was expected to share insights on the future of digital marketing.

As Alex began his presentation, it became evident that he was using non-inclusive language. He consistently used "I" and "my" to describe strategies and experiences, creating a sense of detachment from the audience.

Instead of connecting with the attendees, his language choices made him appear self-centered and distant. For instance, he stated, "In my experience, I've found that my approach to marketing has always been successful." This continuous use of "I" isolated the audience, who had hoped to gain insights applicable to their own situations.

As the presentation continued, attendees grew increasingly disengaged. The lack of relatable examples and the focus on Alex's individual achievements disconnected the audience from the message.

When the presentation ended, there was a Q&A session. During this session, Alex was surprised to notice that he was not asked many questions, and the audience was not connecting with him.

When the organizers collected informal feedback on Alex's presentation, many people in the audience gave feedback that they felt Alex was "too much in love with himself."

In hindsight, Alex realized the impact of his language choices. By using non-inclusive language, he had missed a valuable opportunity to connect with his audience and share insights that could benefit a diverse range of professionals.

Very often, business leaders like Alex can struggle with this issue. They can have a very strong focus on themselves as individuals, which reflects in the language they use while presenting. When the language becomes increasingly "I-focused," the audience quickly realizes and starts disengaging with the person.

The issue is that this happens unconsciously. The presenter doesn't even realize the impression that they are creating!

Let's go back to Barack Obama.

Obama is known for his speeches as being inclusive. One of the ways that he does this is by using the word "We" more than "I."

In his victory speech on election night in 2008, he effectively used "we" to emphasize inclusiveness. Here's an excerpt from that speech:

> *"It's been a long time coming, but tonight, because of what we did on this day, in this election, at this defining moment, change has come to America. A little bit earlier this evening, I received an extraordinarily gracious call from Senator McCain. Senator McCain fought long and hard in this campaign. And he's fought even longer and harder for the country that he loves. He has endured sacrifices for America that most of us cannot begin to imagine. We are better off for the service rendered by this brave and selfless leader."*

In this excerpt, Obama uses "we" to convey a sense of shared accomplishment and to emphasize the collective effort that led to his election victory.

Additionally, by acknowledging both his supporters and his opponent, he demonstrates unity and the idea that the journey to change was a collective one.

In fact, in the entire approx. 26-minute speech, Obama used "I" only about 11 times and used "We" 23 times!

But is inclusive language only about replacing I with We? Obviously not! Inclusive language also means taking everyone together. It involves making everyone feel that they are all a part of one team, even if sometimes they may have different viewpoints.

A few years ago, I was coaching a senior business leader. The role of this leader was to influence sales teams in various geographies to sell products & services offered by this business leader's vertical. Her entire success depended upon her ability to influence the sales team and build relationships with them.

During our coaching engagement, this leader pointed out to me the issues she was seeing with the sales team. She mentioned that the sales team was not taking the initiative to sell the vertical's solutions to the market. She also felt that many of them lacked knowledge and general responsiveness. She shared her frustration with me.

As a part of the coaching process, I had the opportunity to watch her interact with the sales team during a meeting. I realized that during the meeting, she did several things to further distance the sales team from her vertical. Here is a list of things I saw her do:

- Several times during the meeting, she made pointed comments on the lack of responsiveness from one particular geography.

- While talking about the opportunities the team had won, she used language suggesting that she was the main reason behind winning those opportunities.

- She frequently used words such as "sales team" and "vertical team," which further cemented the silos.

- Her tone while talking to the team was also very condescending.

As expected, the listeners also reacted to her approach accordingly. They made comments that the "vertical team" was not close to the ground reality. They started mentioning instances of lack of support from her team. The list went on…

A few days after the meeting, I set up a coaching session with this leader. I spoke to her about the need to be inclusive and asked her to reflect on what behaviors she displayed that distanced her stakeholders.

With all credit to her, we had a very authentic conversation, and we were able to generate a list of avoidable behaviors. We then applied the process of "feed forward." We discussed her future meetings with the sales team and the changes in her approach she would incorporate to make people feel included. We identified a list of 4-5 very specific ideas that she would try.

Her next meeting was much better. During that meeting, she was a lot more inclusive. She refrained from taking credit for the success; instead, she gave the team credit for success on some opportunities. She then went on to share a list of "shared opportunities and challenges" and proposed a joint action plan, highlighting the support she can provide.

She refrained from making any personal attacks in the meeting and dealt with all feedback given to her with grace and confidence.

Overall result was that the meeting went much better than her previous meeting, and stakeholder alignment increased.

By **deliberately** focusing on being inclusive, her AURA as a leader was enhanced!

As we reflect on the stories shared, here are some guidelines to keep in mind:

Replace I with We:

Wherever possible, replace I with We. By doing so, as a speaker, you are one with the audience. Reflect on whether you have a default tendency to use I in your presentations. Identify specific areas in your communication where you would like to replace I with We.

Acknowledge Diversity:

Recognize the diversity of your audience by using examples, anecdotes, or references that resonate with different backgrounds and perspectives. Before communicating with an audience, take out some time to reflect on their profile. Consider how you will communicate the messages to them.

Don't Disregard Sensitivity:

Be sensitive to cultural, social, or political sensitivities. Avoid topics, language, or imagery that could inadvertently offend or marginalize certain groups.

Avoid Using Phrases That Exclude People:

As much as possible, avoid using phrases that may make people feel excluded. Stay away from phrases that imply distance, such as "you wouldn't understand" or "some of you are too young to know", "XYZ team is like this."

Avoid Taking Solo Credit:

When talking about achievements, avoid using language that reinforces the perception that you are taking solo credit. Share names and contributions of other people. Deliberately look for opportunities to share credit with others. A little recognition in the course of communication can make people feel included.

Watch The Tone:

Reflect on whether you can sometimes have a condescending tone. The tone of our voice communicates emotions. Specifically, avoid using any type of tone that may demean others.

Leverage Partnership Words:

Partnership words are words that indicate a partnership between the speakers and the listeners. These words indicate that both the speaker and the listener belong to the same level and to the same team. Some of the best partnership words are:

Our….

Shared…

Together…

Joint….

Think about how you can leverage these words in your presentation. Be deliberate about using this language.

Avoid Negative Stereotyping:

As much as possible, avoid the tendency to negatively stereotype a group. This can happen unconsciously through language, such as:

"ABC team is operating differently than the others," or "X function needs to support B function more."

Obviously, the journey toward using more inclusive language starts with self-awareness of where you currently are. Here is a quick self-assessment you can take:

Inclusive Language Assessment

Please rate yourself on a scale of 1 to 5 on the following criteria, where 1 indicates "Strongly Disagree" and 5 indicates "Strongly Agree."

Criteria	1	2	3	4	5
Replace 'I' with 'We': I consistently use 'We' more than 'I' in the presentations that I make.					
Acknowledge Diversity: I consciously analyse the diversity of my audience and use examples, anecdotes, or references that resonate with different backgrounds and perspectives.					
Sensitivity: I am sensitive to cultural, social, or political nuances of the audience. I avoid language or imagery that could inadvertently offend or marginalize certain groups.					
Avoid Using Phrases That Exclude: I consciously avoid using phrases that can exclude others.					
Share Credit: During presentations and conversations, I don't use language that implies solo credit.					
Tone: During meetings, my tone is not condescending to others.					
Leverage Partnership Words: I consciously leverage partnership words and language in my presentations.					
Negative Stereotyping: I avoid doing any kind of negative stereotyping.					

Technique 7: Stories

One of the most memorable books that I have read is *Roots*. This book is a story of a family of slaves in the U.S. who are trying to ensure that, as a new generation is born, they understand the roots of "where they come from."

The protagonists use stories of family history and anecdotes, which are passed down across generations, to do this.

Stories have been used throughout history to share knowledge, culture, and to inspire others. Stories have been one of the most powerful ways that we, as humans, use to communicate and connect with others.

The origins of stories date back to prehistoric times when humans gathered around campfires to share experiences. Then, with the advent of writing, stories started coming together in scrolls and books, making it easier to ensure that messages live for centuries.

In today's digital and technology-enabled world, we have stories all around us. They are everywhere, in all social media, and they stick!

Leaders who are able to evoke emotions of others are purposeful in using stories to communicate their message and inspire others.

Business storytelling is also about being able to communicate complex messages, like a story, so that people remember.

Jan Carlzon, the legendary ex-CEO of SAS, has been one of the leaders whose work has inspired me. While the work he did was far deeper (and wider) than storytelling, the way he cascaded the SAS strategy like a story to all employees is a case study in itself.

Here is a brief on the problem statement and how storytelling was deployed:

SAS, as an airline, was facing very turbulent market conditions. The organization was struggling against rising competition, high fuel costs, along with several internal cultural challenges.

During this time, Jan Carzlon, along with his leadership team, created a strong strategy focused on customer experience and on-time performance. One of the core issues they were facing was ensuring deployment and common understanding of the strategy across the organization.

To enable this, the organization decided to create and cascade "The Little Red Book of SAS." In this visually appealing book, the leadership team communicated the strategy through a storytelling approach. To explain the story, they used little text but a lot of visual imagery to ensure simplicity (but clarity) of the message.

The story started with pictures of how in the past SAS was on a growth path with favorable conditions. It then explained how "turbulent market conditions" had hit the airline, with rising fuel costs, more competition, and several other factors.

Then, the story further unfolded as it mentioned the financial condition of the organization. Once these critical contextual messages were communicated, the little red book then focused on the future and mentioned pictorially the financial goals for the next year. It then mentioned critical success factors to ensure that the organization delivers on the desired numbers.

The story followed beautifully to then link desirable employee behaviors to support the strategy and the need of special projects, like "project punctuality", to deliver a consistent, on-time performance.

In more than 2 decades that I have been in consulting, I haven't seen a better example of communicating strategy as a story and making complex messages simple!

When you get a chance, do a search for "Little Red Book of SAS" so that you can experience what I have tried to articulate.

The interesting thing is that stories, when well communicated, create an experience for the audience! When we experience something powerful, we remember it for a long time.

How to structure a story?

To develop and structure a story, I would recommend us to follow the S.T.O.R.Y framework below. This framework explains the key elements of a story (in a chronological order) and helps us to develop and articulate inspiring stories.

- **S - Situation:** All good stories start with explaining the situation. The situation covers the background of the story and critical context that the audience must know about. In the case of SAS, this was the background of high growth that the organization had experienced in the past.

- **T-Tension:** Once the situation is covered, a powerful story then moves to a tension point. In SAS's case, this was the turbulent market conditions and associated financial condition. Tension comprises the core issue that the protagonist was/is dealing with.

- **O-Occurrence:** Simply put, this section of the story covers actions that were taken after the tension. In a future-focused story, this step can also include "what do we need to do." Jan Carlzon covered this through a focus on key priorities.

- **R-Results:** Stories need a strong ending, and therefore, it's critical for people to visualize the result of the actions. Results, therefore, consist of how the story ended and what eventually unfolded.

- **Your Takeaway:** We have heard this many times – "moral of the story is…" Therefore, finally, any good story will have a discussion on strong takeaways and reflections. In the case of SAS, this was covered as a set of employee behaviors.

Let's take an example of the S.T.O.R.Y. framework in action.

A few years ago, I was working with a senior executive in a large firm. One of the issues he was dealing with was the lack of collaboration within his team, which was impacting the team outputs and the team's perception.

He mentioned to me the challenge and explained that he was planning a team offsite to have authentic conversations around team collaboration issues and create an action plan.

We discussed possible ways and techniques to facilitate the conversation so that it becomes a shared action plan. While discussing the same, I mentioned to him about the power of stories and encouraged him to consider a real-life story that he can share at the start of the meeting to set the context.

He shared with me many possible stories from the "generic world", but I encouraged him to think about an actual real story that had happened to him. I explained to him that if he shared a real-life story, he would be able to articulate the messages better and evoke emotions in an authentic manner.

On the day of the team offsite meeting, this executive shared a very powerful story with his team.

This story dates back to the early years of his career when he was a team member within the HR function of an organization and how that HR team came together to delight their internal customer.

Here, he applied the S.T.O.R.Y framework:

Situation:

He started the story by explaining that 15 years ago he was a member of the HR team of an organization. He mentioned that the perception of the HR team within the organization was very bureaucratic and slow. This was impacting the motivation level of the entire team.

Tension:

He then mentioned that one of the key issues why this was happening was because within the HR team, various sub-functions were operating as mini-fiefdoms, with a focus on traditional HR metrics that were not internally customer-focused.

Occurrence:

He then elaborated that a new leader came to head the function, and they all went for a similar offsite. He mentioned that in this offsite, the leader requested the team to not focus on individual functions but work with a vision to be the most customer-centric HR team.

With this vision, during the 2 days, they brainstormed on "what does the customer want," "what should the new KPIs be," and "how do we create a perception of one team which is obsessed with customers."

The team developed a strong charter and action plan. This was then followed by sincere execution and pitstop sessions. The team developed new stretch SLAs because that's what the business needed.

Results:

The above actions led to some very strong positive results for the team. He mentioned that within his organization, this team got recognized as the most customer-centric HR team. Equally importantly, some of the innovative work that the team did served the organization for years to come.

Your Takeaway:

Finally, he mentioned that when he looks back at his career, he is proud of what the team achieved, and he is honored to say, "I was a member of that team." He mentioned that this experience made him realize the true power of teamwork, which is immeasurable pride even years after this incident happened.

What a powerful, contextual story! You can imagine the impact a story like this would have had at the start of the team meeting. We can be sure that it would have inspired many people, if not all.

Storytelling Affects the Brain:

One of the reasons to add storytelling to your executive presence toolbox is because there is enough scientific research that has proven that storytelling affects and engages the brain of the listener.

When people listen to an impactful story, there are high chances that they will not just remember the same but also retell that story to others.

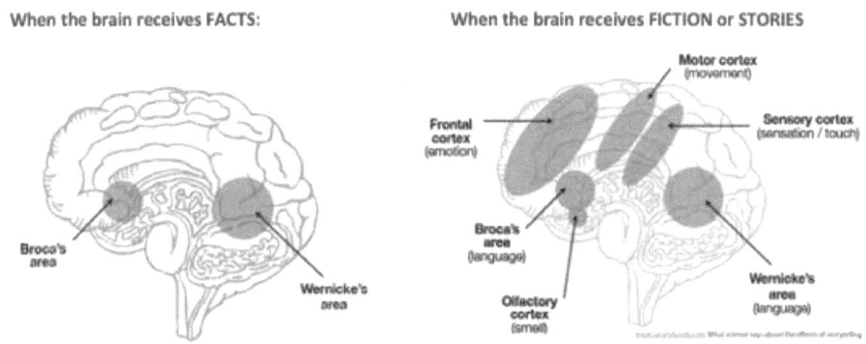

When we retell a story, we have perceived, comprehended, and interpreted the ideas/thoughts gained from the story.

This deepens connections within various regions in our brain, and as this cycle continues, the story gets consolidated into long-term memory (just like the Jan Carlzon story is now embedded in my long-term memory).

This can then lead to "neural coupling." What this means is that when someone *hears* a story, their brain lights up in the same way as the speaker's brain when they are *telling* the story.

There is a fair amount of research available in this area. In fact, research has also pointed out that when our brain hears stories, many parts of the brain get activated as opposed to when we hear facts.

Therefore, next time you have to inspire someone, leave a message that sticks, or energize your audience - Think S.T.O.R.Y!

Reflection Exercise:

Think about the following situation and an apt story for the same:

"One of the members in your team has been struggling to achieve her goals. Because of that, she is feeling demotivated and anxious." Put down below what story can you share:

Framework	Key Question	Response
Situation	What was the situation happening, and with whom?	
Tense	What were 1-2 key tension points?	
Occurrence	What happened next? What did the protagonist do?	
Results	What was the impact of their actions?	
Your Takeaway	What is the core learning?	

Key Guidelines for Telling Stories:

Here are some key guidelines to keep in mind while sharing stories:

1. **Real life:** Real-life stories have a lot more impact than functional stories. As much as possible, share stories that have happened in real life, especially anecdotes that have happened to you.

2. **Match the context:** Ensure the story that you share is relevant to the context of the situation. Out-of-context stories have little to no impact on the listener.

3. **Keep them short:** Business stories are not long. Keep them precise, to the point, and short. Typically, a good story lasts 4-5 minutes on the outside.

4. **Modulate your voice:** Use your voice as a tool to create drama, tension points, and "aha" moments. More on voice modulation is given later in this book.

5. **Relatable:** Share stories of characters and places that your audience can relate to. This can help them to visualize better.

6. **Keep them light:** While stories can convey serious messages, the actual delivery of stories should be kept light. This helps the audience feel engaged and listen to them in a non-threatening manner.

7. **Follow the framework:** For higher chances of success, follow the S.T.O.R.Y. framework!

Technique 8: Contrast

A few years ago, I had a meeting with the Business Head of a large firm. This organization was going through a strategic change that required the leadership to think and operate differently. The purpose of the meeting was for the Business Head to explain to me the old vs. new strategy and expectations from leaders.

During the meeting, the Business Head mentioned to me that in the last 2-3 years, the organization was focusing on cost management. Therefore, their strategy was focused on optimization.

He explained that, therefore, they drove the "optimization mindset" within the leadership team, in which each leader was constantly looking at ways to reduce cost.

He then mentioned that their organization is now "shifting gears," and the focus has shifted to growth. He mentioned that, therefore, the new strategy needed the leadership to work with a "growth mindset" and look at more growth/value-creating opportunities rather than cost management.

To explain this further, he gave me a very powerful example. He said, "The situation is something like this: In the last 2 years, we have been telling our team that we need to repair our car. Therefore, we have focused on repairing our car by fixing the parts that were not working. We repaired the needed dents, cleaned the scratches, and changed faulty parts. But now we need to change our car. We don't need to repair the car anymore but fundamentally drive a Formula 1 car to accelerate revenue growth velocity. The issue is that our leaders are now used to repairing the old car strategy, whereas we now want them to think Formula 1."

These messages stuck well with me. Through the language that he used, I could completely understand the mission ahead and where I needed to help the team.

I left the meeting supercharged with ideas and excitement!

The example above covers the technique of "contrast" in action. Simply put, contrast is a technique that explains the difference between things or ideas to communicate effectively with the audience. When the leader compared the old strategy vs. the new strategy and then used cars as an analogy, I could easily understand the ask.

As you can notice, using contrast as a strategy has many advantages. Some of them include:

- **Clarity:** Contrasting helps to highlight key differences between ideas, so that the audience can understand.

- **Stickiness:** This technique increases the chances that the listeners will remember the key points, particularly if contrast is combined with analogy.

- **Evokes Emotions:** Contrasting, if done well, evokes "action emotions" in others and inspires them to act.

- **Influencing:** Contrast helps us to build more persuasive arguments, influencing other people.

- **Context:** Particularly, in change, contrast as a technique helps people understand the context of change and also what needs to be changed.

While developing contrasts, here are some key tips that you can keep in mind:

1. **Identify the key points and the messages you want to convey:** In the example above, the leader wanted to communicate the change that the organization was going through and its implications.

2. **Clearly articulate the contrasts:** Clearly articulate and identify the contrasts that are most relevant to the situation.

3. **Rule of 2:** Ideally, identify 2 specific contrasts that you want to highlight.

4. **Examples / Analogies:** Think about supporting the contrast with examples or analogies that you can use to explain your message.

5. **Share them like a story:** Use the storytelling approach covered previously, so that you can communicate contrasts as a story.

6. **Combine other techniques:** Contrast can come to life more specifically when you combine them with 2-3 other techniques covered in this book.

Here is an example of point 6 above:

A few years ago, I was consulting a client who was a senior leader in a large established organization. Like several large organizations, this organization was relatively slow in innovation.

The market conditions had changed. Many new start-ups had entered their industry, and therefore, the leadership team in this organization needed to relook at their innovation process to make it more agile and faster.

The business leader and I decided to conduct an offsite workshop with the core leadership team to help them understand this change and develop a new innovation process.

We specifically discussed what messages he would give at the start of the workshop to clearly articulate the change needed.

As we were brainstorming, I shared contrast as a technique with him and asked him to consider how he can leverage the same.

He promised to give it some thought and be prepared accordingly. At the start of the offsite, he shared the following:

"Everyone, as you are aware, we have together built a strong established brand in the market. Our brand stands for a good reputation, and we have been enjoying a strong market share.

Our customers have acknowledged the work we all do, but as our loyalists, they have also given us one feedback: We need to bring out innovative products and fresh ideas faster.

One of our key accounts has candidly shared with us that they now perceive us to be an Elephant. While we are considered dependable and stable, they consider us as too slow.

The feedback that they have shared with us is that we need to be more like Leopards - fast, agile, and responsive.

This is the challenge we are here to solve today!

We need to discuss our process of innovation. We need to discuss what process we want to follow so that our customers and employees can see a visible change in us. We need to discuss what actions will make our organization an innovative Leopard."

The leader was able to articulate his message well, and contrast as a strategy had worked well to set the tone for a highly energized discussion. We had activated "action emotions."

Here is a question: read through the above story once more and ask yourself, what other techniques were used apart from contrast by the leader?

Can you spot at least 3 more?

You are right! Apart from contrast, the leader used analogy, anaphora, and inclusive language!

This is the power of these techniques. When you combine them together, you have a multiplying effect on the impact of your communication.

Technique 9: Voice Modulation

One of the most uninspiring presentations I witnessed was from the CEO of a company sharing the company's strategy during an all-employee meeting.

This organization was going through a major change, and the CEO had to communicate that change and the new strategy to all the employees. During the presentation, the CEO had very low energy and used a flat tone of voice to communicate the strategy.

There was no excitement in his voice, and he delivered a "lecture" that would be hard to remember. His voice lacked emphasis in key points, and frankly, he could not energize his audience.

It was not that the CEO did not believe in the strategy; he did. He had spent months contemplating the strategic direction along with his leadership team, but he just lacked the executive presence to cascade the same.

One of the key roadblocks toward executive presence is when the presenter does not leverage a very critical asset – "Their Voice!"

Our voice is one of the key tools to deliver messages with impact. Modulating our voice while presenting has a lasting impact on energizing the audience.

Voice modulation is our ability to adjust our voice, so that we can deliver memorable messages. There are some people who are naturally gifted with this skill, but many others have to learn this skill.

Here are some very practical tips to keep in mind for effective voice modulation:

Focus on Critical Words:

While preparing for a presentation, think about the words that you would use to deliver a message. From the list of words, identify the most critical words that you would need to emphasize. Let's look at the words below as an example:

> "Today, let's talk about the new direction we need to take. We have bold ambitions, and this new strategy can help us to get there faster."

Now, imagine the impact on the listeners if the speaker adds emphasis to the highlighted words:

> "Today, let's talk about the **new direction** we need to take. We have **bold ambitions**, and this **new** strategy can help us to get there **faster**."

Just by focusing on some critical words, the impact of the message is greatly enhanced!

Manage Energy:

Personal energy of the speaker goes a long way to inspire their audience. If the speaker has low energy while presenting, they can find it difficult to engage the audience.

Similarly, if the energy is too high, many audience members can get disconnected. Therefore, it is important to maintain a strong "energy balance" while presenting.

I have found that speakers who have good executive presence generally have moderately high energy levels while presenting, but they "raise their energy" while presenting some very specific points!

Let's work through the example we used earlier:

"Today, let's talk about the **new direction** we need to take. We have **bold ambitions**, and this **new** strategy can help us to get there **faster**. To do this, we need to do 3 things:

- **Number One:** We need to drive more innovation.

- **Number Two:** We should be **obsessed with customers.**

- **Number Three:** We need to bust silos.

Imagine if the presenter in the above example is laying emphasis on the highlighted words and also increasing their energy!

Use Strategic Pauses:

Another important tip is to use a strategic pause after making a critical point, or when you are about to make one. As shared earlier, strategic pauses are soft, 2-3-second pauses that drive the impact. Let's now see this in action below.

"Today, let's talk about the **new direction** we need to take (**strategic pause**). We have **bold ambitions**, and this **new** strategy can help us to get there **faster** (strategic pause). To do this, we need to do 3 things:

- **Number One (Strategic pause):** We need to **drive** more innovation

- **Number Two (Strategic pause):** We should be **obsessed with customers.**

- **Number Three:** We need to bust silos!

By using strategic pauses, the impact of the speaker increases dramatically!

Pace of Speech:

Another rule of thumb that I would recommend is that when in doubt, use a moderate pace of speech. Many people are naturally fast speakers, and their pace of talking is quick. Some others have a slow natural pace of talking.

For most presentations, I have realized that a moderate pace of speech is the most appropriate.

Express Emotions in Voice:

Finally, another important point to consider is to express the emotion through your voice.

When we are delivering a message and using words, our tone of talking must express the emotions that the words are intending to express.

So, if our words are intending to communicate excitement, our voice should be excited! If our words want to communicate urgency, our voice must communicate the same.

Let's do a quick exercise on this:

1. **Read through the sentence below:.**

   Today, let's talk about the **new direction** we need to take. We have **bold ambitions**, and this **new** strategy can help us to get there **faster**. To do this, we need to do 3 things:

   o **Number One:** We need to drive more innovation.

   o Number Two: We should be **obsessed with customers**.

   o **Number Three:** We need to **bust silos.**

2. Now, imagine that your goal is to communicate excitement. Say the words with an excited voice.

3. Now, imagine that your goal is to create urgency. Say the words with urgency in your voice!

You would have noticed that when you said the words with the goal of creating excitement, your face would have lit up. Maybe you smiled while saying these words, and maybe your pauses were a bit longer.

Similarly, while saying the same words to communicate urgency, something different may have happened. Maybe you were not smiling anymore, and your pace of speech became faster?

The beauty of this technique is that it answers a very specific question:

> **"What emotions do I want my audience to feel while sharing this message?"**

When you are clear about what emotions you want to evoke, tone modulation happens automatically!

Practice Time:

Please see below the text of one of the business leader's messages that I had shared earlier. As you read this, put an _____ below words where you will need to put more emphasis and put a! for sections where you will take a strategic pause:

"Everyone, as you are aware, we have together built a strong established brand in the market. Our brand stands for a good reputation, and we have been enjoying a strong market share.

Our customers have acknowledged the work we all do, but as our loyalists, they have also given us one feedback: We need to bring out innovative products and fresh ideas faster.

One of our key accounts has candidly shared with us that they now perceive us to be an Elephant. While we are considered dependable and stable, they consider us as too slow.

The feedback that they have shared with us is that we need to be more like Leopards - fast, agile, and responsive.

This is the challenge we are here to solve today!

We need to discuss our process of innovation. We need to discuss what process we want to follow so that our customers and employees can see a visible change in us. We need to discuss what actions will make our organization an innovative Leopard."

Technique 10: Managing Butterflies!

"I have a big presentation to make in my office and I am feeling really anxious about it." One of my friends shared this with me a couple of days before the "Big" presentation.

It is very human to feel butterflies of anxiety before a presentation. Almost all of us would have felt it at some point and some of us continue to feel it (even after making hundreds of presentations).

While I will share some very practical tips on how to manage anxiety, at the outset, let's consider how it is good for us!

Feeling anxious is good for us because it helps us to prepare better by:

- Helping us to imagine various messages of our communication and deciding how to deliver them.

- Motivates us to do that extra research on the topic and builds deeper knowledge on the subject area.

- Makes us want to inspire others and do a good job!

During the course of my experience, I have found that leaders with executive presence use the following practices to manage anxiety and stage fear:

Understand the source of anxiety:

When we feel anxious before the presentation, it's a good practice to take a pause and simply ask yourself, "What is causing me to feel like this?"

There are typically 2 types of answers that may come out:

a. You may be feeling anxious because you are under-prepared on the subject. There may be parts of the content that you are not comfortable with. If this is the issue, extra research and preparation can help resolve the issue.

b. You are well prepared on the content, but your mind is playing distortions with you!

Be Aware of Cognitive Distortions:

Cognitive distortions are "internal silent scripts" that we experience sometimes before a presentation. These distortions are mostly not real and are like mini-games that our mind plays with us. Being aware of cognitive distortions that most likely may impact you is helpful.

Let's do an activity. Given below is a checklist of cognitive distortions. Go through the same and select the ones that apply to you:

Checklist of cognitive distortions

Distortion	Description	Does this happen with me?
Worst Case Scenario,	Imagining a worst-case scenario that you will not do a good job.	
Negative Audience Bias.	Assuming that your audience will react negatively to your messages,	
Audience Capability Bias	Assuming that your listeners are either more capable or less capable than you,	
Past Incidents	Overthinking past incidents where you did not present well,	
Imagining Issues	Imagining that you will face multiple issues while presenting (including logistics, technology, etc),	
Feeling Judged	Overthinking that you will be judged and evaluated on the basis of your presentation.	
Being The Best	Wanting to be the best presenter "out there."	

Once you are aware of the cognitive distortion that you are facing, your mind will "self-coach" you on the process of managing/balancing the distortion!

Here are some helpful strategies to manage these:

Distortion	Negative Description.	Helpful Strategy
Worst Case Scenario,	Imagining a worst-case scenario that you will not do a good job.	"Catch yourself" imagining the worst-case scenario and ask yourself, "I hope I am not being too negative."
Negative Audience Bias.	Assuming that your audience will react negatively to your messages,	Make a list of the audience who you believe will definitely be positive. Assume that people will be balanced!
Audience Capability Bias	Assuming that your listeners are either more capable or less capable than you,	Simply ask, "Do I have real data to support this?"
Past Incidents	Overthinking past incidents where you did not present well,	Focus on how you will apply learnings from the past.
Imagining Issues	Imagining that you will face multiple issues while presenting (including logistics, technology, etc),	Make a list of issues that you can face, and address the ones that you think you have not thought about!
Feeling Judged	Overthinking that you will be judged and evaluated on the basis of your presentation.	Replace thinking with – How can I create the best value for the audience.
Being The Best	Wanting to be the best presenter "out there."	Tell yourself, it's not a do-or-die competition!

Focus on start:

One of the things that I always advise people on is to focus on having a good start. If your first 5 minutes go well, you will build enough comfort to carry you through the rest. For example, one of the presenters that I know likes to always start his presentations with a question.

He feels that by asking the audience a question at the start, he is able to engage with them and calm his nerves.

Here are some examples of "techniques in the first 5 minutes" that I have seen good presenters use to "calm themselves":

- Starting with a question.

- Sharing a story.

- Opening with a video,

- Having a poll or rhetorical question.

- Sharing a humorous self-introduction.

- Picking a message from the previous speaker and then linking their topic to the same.

Think about what your "go-to technique" can be for the first 5 minutes!

Know the Logistics and Technology:

Surprise during presentations on logistics/technology is not a great thing. If logistically things don't go as planned, it can put a presenter in a very anxious situation.

I have seen that leaders with good executive presence manage this through some very simple practices:

- Reaching the venue much before time to understand the room layout.

- Testing technology a few times before getting started.

- Having a backup plan in case there are technology challenges.

- Making a mental note of logistical challenges they can face during the presentation, and being prepared to handle the audience if these challenges happen.

Carry Joy Nudges:

I learned this technique through one of my friends. We were talking about techniques to manage stage fear, and he mentioned something very powerful to me.

He said his daughter loves to draw, and watching her draw has a calming effect on him. He mentioned that once when he was very nervous about a presentation and wanted to calm himself down. So, he carried one of his daughter's drawing brushes with him so that, while presenting, he could see the brush.

Just the act of seeing the brush while presenting made him realize the joy in his life, and suddenly, all nervousness disappeared!

Simply, this technique means that sometimes, while presenting, if we remember the little moments of joy in our life, we can manage anxiety better.

Think about which joy nudge you can carry! Maybe it's that book that you are reading, or maybe it is that pen that someone close to you has gifted you. It can be anything, just something that nudges you to see the joy!

Anticipate Questions:

One of the key sources of anxiety can also be tough questions that you can face during a presentation. The best way to manage is to prepare for them! Put yourself in the audience's shoes and ask yourself, "If I was listening to this presentation, what questions will come to my mind?" Make a list of 8-10 tough questions that the audience is likely to ask and prepare their responses in advance.

Memorize:

Finally, to manage anxiety, it is absolutely critical for you to memorize the presentation. This means remembering the content in detail. If it's a PowerPoint presentation, then this means remembering which slide comes after which slide. If it's a speech, it's about remembering which message will come after what message.

One of the best tools that I found for this is mind mapping. While, I will not cover mind mapping in detail, it's a very structured way for creative thinking, brainstorming ideas, and developing your thoughts.

From a communication perspective, mind mapping involves creating a one-pager of your communication/presentation.

The sections are created in a chronological manner, so that your mind remembers what to cover when. Here is an example of what mind maps for a presentation can look like:

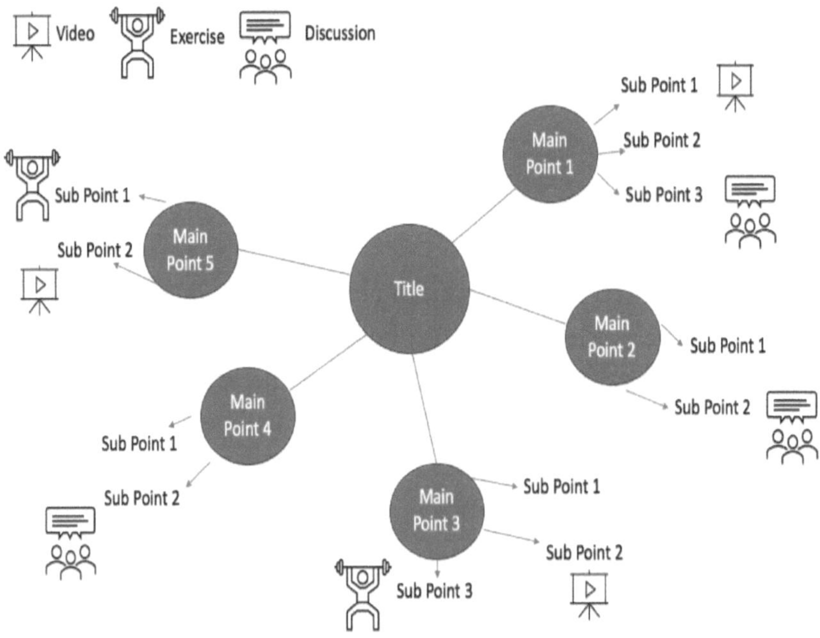

Here are some simple instructions on how to use this:

1. Put the topic/title of the presentation in the middle.

2. Consider all the "main points" you want to make. Main points can be main messages or key slides that you will be sharing.

3. Put main point 1 at the top right-hand corner, the next main point after that, and so on.

4. For each main point, consider the subpoints. These will be smaller messages or arguments within the main point.

5. Then, for each subpoint, **consider the technique**. Use **symbols to remember** where you would give an example, and where you would show a video, etc.

Use this technique before any presentation or communication, and chances are that you will not forget the flow!

Not only that, by having such a one-pager in front of you while presenting, you would remember what you have covered and what to do next!

Summary

- Aura can be developed by using some very specific techniques in our communication.

- **Metaphor is a figure of speech in which a word or phrase is applied to an object or action. It is a way of describing something or someone by showing their similarity with something else. When using metaphors, consider the following:**

  - Relevance: Is the metaphor I am planning to use relevant in this situation?

  - Stickiness: Is this metaphor powerful enough for people to remember?

  - Simplicity: Can the metaphor communicate the message in a simple manner?

- Analogy is a comparison between one thing and another, typically for the purpose of explanation or clarification. Unlike a metaphor, the point of an analogy is not merely to *show*, but also to *explain*. Therefore, an analogy follows an explanation on why you are making a comparison so that people can understand.

- **Anaphora is a rhetorical device used in writing and speaking, where a word or phrase is repeated at the beginning of successive sentences, clauses, or phrases. It is a powerful technique that adds emphasis, rhythm, and emotional impact to the message. Key tips to keep in mind:**

  - Identify the key idea or theme.

  - Choose a repeating word or phrase.

  - Use parallel sentence structures.

  - Start sentences with the repeated word or phrase.

  - Avoid overuse.

  - Practice reading aloud.

- Numbers have a unique ability to capture attention, provide structure, and make information more memorable. When used strategically, numbering can transform ordinary communication into impactful and persuasive messages that resonate with the audience..

- Rhetorical questions serve as powerful attention-grabbers as they immediately capture an audience's focus. This engagement is especially valuable in presentations and conversations where the goal is to make a lasting impression. By presenting the information in the form of a question, we are able to engage the audience in a journey of discovery. They create curiosity and increase the chances of retention of the message.

- **One of the most critical issues to watch out for is how much, as a speaker, you have a tendency to use non-inclusive language. Key guidelines to keep in mind:**

  - Replace 'I' with 'We'.

  - Acknowledge Diversity.

  - Don't Disregard Sensitivity.

  - Avoid Using Exclusive Phrases.

  - Avoid Taking Solo Credit.

- **Stories have been used throughout history to share knowledge, culture, and inspire others. Stories have been one of the most powerful ways that we, as humans, use to communicate and connect with others. The S.T.O.R.Y framework covers:**

  - Situation.

  - Tension,

  - Occurrence.

  - Result.

  - Your Takeaway.

- **Contract is a technique that explains the difference between things or ideas to communicate effectively with the audience. Guidelines for developing contrasts:**
  - Identify the key points and the messages you want to convey.
  - Clearly articulate the contrasts.
  - Rule of 2.
  - Examples, Analogies
  - Share them like a story.

- **Voice modulation is our ability to adjust our voice so that we can deliver memorable messages. To do this:**
  - Focus on critical words.
  - Manage energy.
  - Use strategic pauses.
  - Moderate your pace of speech.
  - Express emotions in voice.

- **It is very human to feel butterflies of anxiety before a presentation. Almost all of us would have felt it at some point, and some of us continue to feel it. Some practices to manage this include:**
  - Understanding the source.
  - Being aware of our cognitive distortions,
  - Focusing on the start.
  - Managing logistics.
  - Carrying joy nudges.
  - Anticipating questions.
  - Memorizing through mind maps.

Part 4

The Three "Ds"

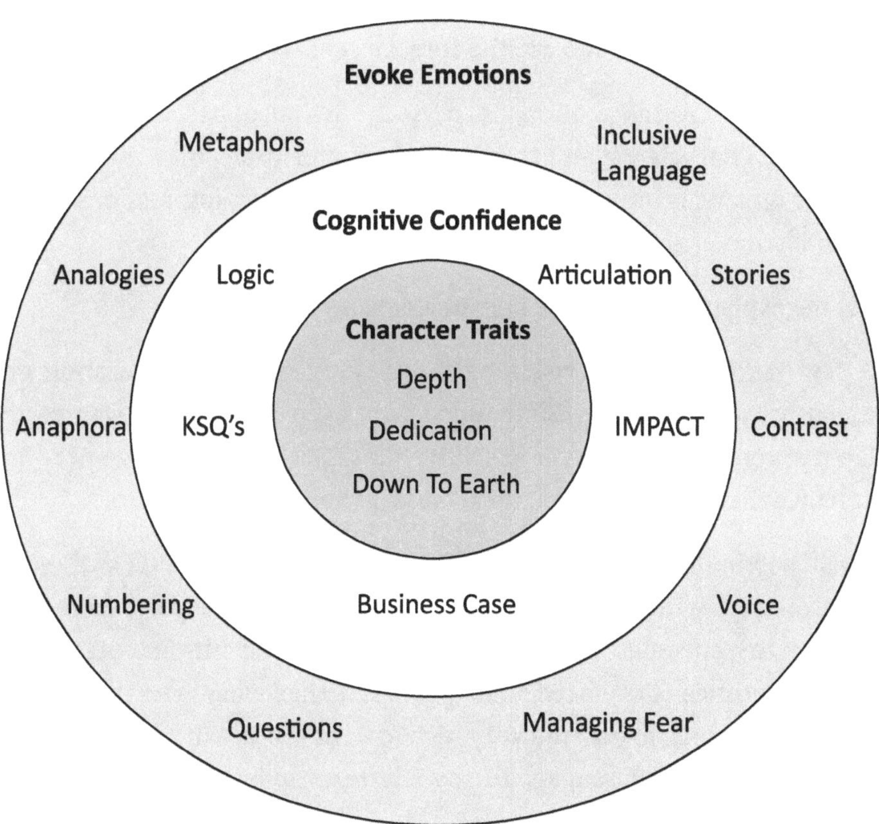

Character Traits: Depth, Dedication and Down to Earth

As we reflect on the sections we have covered earlier, they raise some very pertinent questions:

1. Is executive presence only superficial, limited to some tips and tricks?

2. Doesn't the character of the individual and who they are also play a significant role?

Whereas, tips and tricks are a very key part of sharpening executive presence, they cannot replace the core, i.e., character traits.

"Wholesome Aura" requires a person who also has a strong and authentic character. If a person lacks character traits, they may still be able to create an impact in some events, but lasting impressions come from character strengths.

Let me explain this with the help of an example.

A few years ago, I was coaching the CXO of a large organization on executive presence. The CXO was a very keen learner and wanted to learn several techniques on executive presence. He felt a huge need to enhance the same. However, there was a problem.

This particular leader had not been able to build authentic relationships with his peers in the organization. In the past, there had been many episodes where people had described him as "arrogant" and sometimes "two-faced." His peers felt that whenever this leader needed support, he became very nice toward them, but once the work was done, he did not engage in any relationship building.

As you can imagine, because of the above, people felt that they could not trust him, and they were not sure on the degree of authenticity.

At the start of the coaching journey, we had conducted a 360 degree assessment for the leader. The 360 degree results validated the issues outlined above. However, the problem was that this leader felt that executive presence was only about presentation techniques!

During the coaching conversations, I had to make him realize that trust worthy character was cornerstone of executive presence and no amount of tips would help him develop executive presence. This needed him to reflect on the feedback from his peers, think in a non-judgmental way and leverage the feedback to transform himself.

It took 2-3 long coaching conversations for this leader to realize that he needed to do some fundamental deep reflection and take courageous (and humble) steps toward self-enhancement. Eventually, the leader did progress (albeit slowly, as it happens in these situations) on building deeper, authentic relationships. It took us almost a year to make significant progress, but I was glad to see him grow as a well-rounded professional.

This brings up some questions:

"What makes people worthy of our trust in a professional setting?"

"What character traits do these people have?"

While studying leaders with executive presence, I have identified 3 innate character traits.

They are:

- Depth.

- Dedication.

- Down To Earth,

Let's explore them in greater detail, one by one.

Depth

I remember, a few years ago, I was having a coaching conversation with a young consultant. This individual used to conduct behavioral training programs for corporates and was receiving mixed feedback scores.

Particularly, the individual was not able to conduct sessions for a mid-senior audience. During the session, this person mentioned to me another colleague who this person took as a role model. She asked me, "What tips and tricks does this person use to get good feedback consistently?"

Almost instantly, my answer was, "It's not tips and tricks, it's the depth that this person has built!"

Dictionary definition of depth is the "Distance between the surface and bottom of anything."

When talking about a topic, it means how much do we really know and understand the same. While leaders with strong executive presence can use tips and techniques to deliver their message more effectively, these techniques are not a replacement of their depth (or lack of it).

Think about any speaker who has truly inspired you on any topic. Chances are that this person has built a fair amount of depth and a certain level of expertise within the area.

Leaders with strong executive presence invest time and energy to develop depth. The subject depth that these individuals have comes from years of hard work in exploring their subject better.

These individuals are actually lifelong learners. They develop interest within specific areas and **then adopt a learning attitude to go deeper.**

Therefore, depth here does mean static knowledge, i.e. understanding a particular area or a concept one time, but it means adopting a lifelong learning attitude to explore that area further.

What stops us from doing this?

Why is it that some people explore the surface of a concept and feel that they have "understood everything," while others delve deep into an area and still feel they can learn more?

What differentiates people with shallow knowledge from people with deep depth?

Here are some behaviors to consider:

Shallow Knowledge	Deep Depth
Feel that knowing a concept is good enough.	Realize that knowing a concept is just the start. It is continuous exploration, which is the key.
Conduct limited reflection within an area.	Take out structured time for reflection. These individuals objectively assess themselves.
Do limited or no reading in their area.	Spend a lot of time reading about their chosen area. Invest time in going deeper by constantly acquiring new knowledge and skills.
Find it hard and irrelevant to draw linkages of unrelated items to their area.	Naturally inclined toward outside-in thinking, i.e., linking new, unrelated items to their area of expertise.
Adopt a know-it-all attitude toward knowledge and feedback.	Adopt a "learn-it-all" mindset.

Derailers to Keep in Mind:

To avoid getting trapped with shallow knowledge, here are some derailers to keep in mind:

- **Not reflecting enough:** Maybe the most crucial derailer is not taking out structured time to reflect. **Lack of reflection can put us into a repetitive pattern of mediocrity.**

- **Ego:** Being egotistical or arrogant about your achievements. Ego of any type blocks a learning mindset.

- **Complacency:** Being too relaxed and not feeling the need to invest in your development.

- **Not internalising feedback:** People with shallow knowledge fall into the trap of not internalising the feedback that they receive. They have a tendency to blame or make excuses whenever they hear feedback.

- **Wrong role models:** Very often, having a role model who does not display a learning attitude is also a major derailer. Selecting the right role model **in pursuit of knowledge** is very critical.

- **Pointing towards years of experience:** While experience is a great source of learning, it does not guarantee that the person continues to learn. Having an internal script that says, "I have XYZ years of experience," is detrimental toward developing depth.

- **Not doing enough research:** One of the other derailers of depth is not conducting enough research on the area that you are interested in. This involves not just basic research, but research across industries and geographies to deepen the understanding of your chosen area.

In order to develop depth, here are a couple of frameworks that I have found useful:

Framework 1

One of the key frameworks that has helped me develop some depth in my field is this 2 by 2 matrix given below.

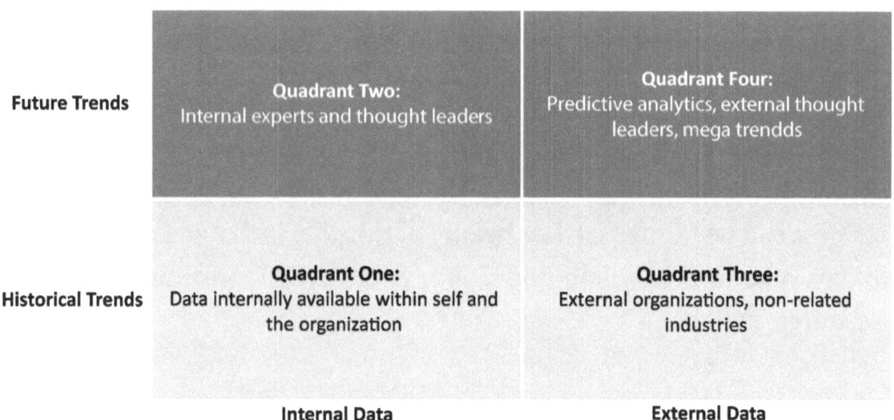

I find this framework to be a very powerful self-awareness tool, which helps me to guide my learning priorities.

Let's say that you are trying to build deeper depth in the area of customer experience. The X-axis here comprises data sources (internal or external). The Y-axis comprises the type of information (historical trends or future trends).

So, in order to develop a deeper depth on the practice of customer experience, I need to look at 4 quadrants:

- **Quadrant 1:** This data is on historical trends of customer experience, and data sources include people who are internal to the organization.

- **Quadrant 2:** This quadrant looks at leveraging internal expertise to develop insights on future CX trends.

- **Quadrant 3:** Here, we look at other external players (including non-industry players) to identify historical trends shaping customer experience.

- **Quadrant 4:** This is a very different ball game. We use this quadrant to leverage the external world to generate insights into future trends.

If we apply a structured approach to understand how customer experience is evolving by using these 4 quadrants, the learning and insights can be immense! The beauty of this tool is that it can be applied to any type of area, including Cyber Security, AI, Insurance, Human Resource, etc.

Most people don't even look at quadrant 1.

The issue is that most people don't even look at quadrant 1! I see several business leaders who do a "cursory glance" at Quadrant 1 and feel that they know enough!

Let's do a quick exercise on this framework.

Reflection Exercise

Identify any one area you want to develop depth in:

____

____

____

____

____

____

____

Quadrants 1 and 2: Think about quadrants 1 and 2 and identify internal sources of expertise that you can leverage to gather insights.

____

____

____

____

____

____

Quadrant 3: Now think of quadrant 3. Identify three things that you can do to generate historical trends from the external ecosystem:

____

____

____

____

____

____

____

Quadrant 4: Identify 3-4 specific activities you can do to identify future trends by immersing yourself in the external ecosystem. At least, 1 of these actions should not be specific to the industry that you are in:

____

____

____

____

____

____

____

Framework 2: Levels of Expertise

Another helpful framework is the levels of expertise given below.

Here is a brief description of all of these 6 levels:

Expert

An expert is someone who has demonstrated sufficient contributions and thought leadership within an area or capability, across most situations, to produce consistent, superior performance overall. In so doing, the person has also developed others in those areas. This person is also considered a true thought leader within their area of focus.

Strength

Strength means that the person has consistently demonstrated their strength in an area. However, they have not yet reached the level of expertise or thought leadership.

Developing Strength

This means that the person has become more proficient in their area and is gradually developing that into a strength. However, there is still more experience required to go to the next level.

Adding Value

Adding value means that the person is like a proficient beginner. They have developed a reasonable level of understanding within an area and can add value to discussions on that area.

Awareness

This means that the person is theoretically aware of an area or capability.

Limitation

Finally, a limitation arises when a person is not even aware of a particular area or capability. They are also sometimes unable to understand why it is a limitation.

This powerful framework helps us to authentically examine our current levels of expertise and decide on a way forward to develop deeper depth. It also serves as a reminder that sometimes, we may feel that we have enough depth on a topic just because we are "aware" or "adding value", but true expertise is far away!

Reflecting with Humility.:

For this framework to work, it is important that we reflect on this with humility. One way to do that is by remembering that we are just lifelong learners! Even someone who is considered an expert by others can still learn!

Back to the example of the young trainer I was mentioning earlier. During our follow-up coaching conversation, I requested this person to choose one area where she wanted to develop expertise and reflect on where she currently was in this framework and where she wanted to be in the next year.

She was authentic enough to acknowledge that, in her area, she was at a "Developing Strength" level.

We then discussed what she could do to increase her strength level over the year and how she would know when she has reached that level.

Overall, she created a great action plan, and I was delighted to see her grow.

I encourage you to apply this tool through the exercise given on the next page.

Reflection Exercise

Choose any one area on which you would like to develop expertise, and answer the questions below:

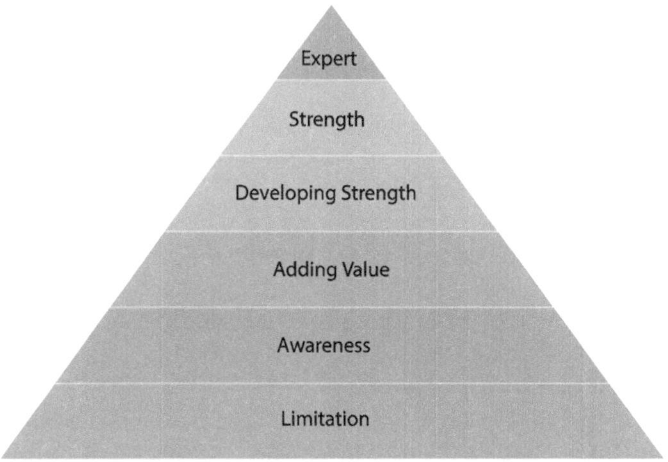

Questions	Response
At what level of expertise do you think you are at today?	
In 1 year, at what level of expertise would you like to reach?	
At what level of expertise would your stakeholders rate you today?	
Specifically, what 3-4 things can you do in the next year to build deeper expertise and visibility in this area?	

Dedication

"It gave me goosebumps," said a friend of mine working in a large organization. He was mentioning a recent town hall meeting in which the CEO of the organization had covered the new strategy. He mentioned that it was "visible" that the CEO was committed and passionate about the new strategy. The CEO's passion was infectious, which made the listeners feel excited and inspired.

Dedication stands for "The quality of being dedicated to a task or a purpose." One of the key character traits of leaders with executive presence is their dedication.

Dedicated individuals are special; they have:

- An inherent sense of purpose, which drives them

- Infectious magnetic energy that draws people to them.

- Passion that inspires others to act.

My friend and his colleagues had experienced dedication in action!

From the perspective of executive presence, dedication is of 2 types:

- Dedication to a task/purpose

- Dedication to help and support others.

Let's take an example to understand this better.

A few years ago, I had a wonderful opportunity to consult an organization that was dedicated to the cause of uplifting the lives of socially underprivileged sections of society. This social enterprise had been founded by a very passionate founder who genuinely wanted to create an ecosystem of entrepreneurs leading large-scale social change.

During my first meeting with her (and many others that followed), I felt really inspired. In the meeting, she spoke about her own background and the impact it had on her to create the social entrepreneurs' ecosystem.

She spoke about her vision for the nation and shared the progress that she and her team were making on the same.

She then covered in detail the issues of scalability and leadership that social entrepreneurs face, and she wanted to create an ecosystem of support for them.

It was visible to me that she was passionate about this area, and by listening to her, I felt the need to be a part of her movement. Her dedication inspired me to think about the challenges that social enterprises face and contribute to their mission in any small way I could. It is a meeting that I would remember.

That is the power of dedication. When you are a dedicated individual, other people notice. They realize that you are a mission-driven individual, and because of this, people feel like interacting with you more and listening to you more.

Dedicated individuals are purpose-driven individuals. They have deep clarity on their purpose and mission. Therefore, they don't need to be trained on tips and tricks. Their passion almost automatically transpires to impactful delivery, strong articulation, and voice modulation.

While not all people may be as cause-driven as the example above, I believe that each one of us can do deeper reflection to find causes that we are dedicated to. Sometimes, we need to nudge ourselves to discover this.

Here are a couple of practices that can support this discovery:

Think About the Superordinate Goal:

Sometimes, when we get busy in the "business as usual" life, we tend to focus more on the transactions rather than the "why" behind them.

In such cases, it's good to take a pause and consider the "superordinate goal."

One of the leaders that I was working with was trying to find a way to align his team to the sales plans for the year. He had put together a comprehensive presentation on the financial numbers, key metrics, and underlying tactics. However, as he took me through the presentation, we both felt that something was missing.

After much discussion, we realised that a superordinate goal/mission was lacking. In this case, we discovered that his business was catering to an underserved demand in the market. It was not just a sales plan but an opportunity to create a new industry-first business line!

I requested him to consider this aspect for 2 reasons:

- To unlock his personal drive,

- To inspire his team, by avoiding the temptation to share just another strategy presentation.

We met a few weeks later after that conversation and I was excited to see the transformation his thinking had gone through. He had connected with a deeper sense of mission to serve a customer base that nobody in the industry was serving. He had uncovered several challenges that he would face to achieve his mission and worked on the plan with a mindset of "conquering the impossible" and "industry-first approach."

He had dramatically changed the messaging of his presentation to reflect this thinking and was feeling much more personally charged and excited to share this with his team!

What we learnt in the process was the power of superordinate goals to:

- Finding purpose in business as usual issues

- Reframe goals into missions

- Unlocking hidden answers to "why,"

- Energizing messaging and impact.

- Creative thinking!

So, next time, you are about to make a presentation which you feel is "regular", take a step back and ask yourself:

"What is the superordinate goal behind this?"

"What is the why?"

Paint a Picture of the Future:

Another way to unlock dedication and superordinate goals is to do some "future backward" thinking. Future backward is a very powerful process in which you paint a written image of the future you are trying to create and use that to define what needs to be done now.

I learned this through one of my friends. This person had just taken on a new role, which involved setting up a new function for an organization.

As it happens, the new function was a "single-person army," which can be quite challenging. During one of our conversations, I asked him, "What inspires you to carry on?" He said, "It's my vision for the function."

He then went on to explain to me how he had created his vision for the function "Two years from now." He had put the vision together in a one-page document, and he mentioned that all the work he does, the presentations he makes, are keeping in mind this vision.

In this case, because my friend had created a vision for the future, he had found a deep source of self-motivation, which was visible to others as well!

As expected, this individual went on to create immense value for himself and his organization.

Focus on Helping Others

Another strong force that can drive dedication is a focus on helping others. Helping others is a very special behavior. Remember the last time you helped someone. It may be a colleague in the office, a friend in need, or even a stranger.

How did you feel about yourself after helping someone? I am sure you felt good, and it created a positive narrative in your mind of who you are. It may have inspired you to focus on helping others more.

When we are focused on helping others, we appeal to our own higher self of maturity and purpose. It helps us to define a reason for what we are doing and helps us to unlock our passion.

One very good example of this is the Head Coach of Boot Camp Yellow (BCY). BCY is a Gurugram-based outdoor fitness training group that helps people become fitter through structured and progressive outdoor training. Jatin is the head coach of BCY, who has truly inspired me.

He has amazing knowledge and depth on the topic. However, to me, he is also a role model of dedication. Here is the way he displays the same:

BCY's vision is, "To be a leader in building community health, providing exceptional and innovative outdoor training program."

Through his actions, words, and role-modeling behavior, Jatin completely role models this vision. He is constantly working with his fellow coaches to develop new and improved programs. He personally invests time to update and upgrade himself on the latest techniques. When you interact with him, you immediately notice that you are interacting with a purpose-driven, inspired individual.

Dedication to support others: While operating the BCY community, it is amazing to see how Jatin is able to find time to give every athlete individual attention.

His dedication is visible as he engages with individuals regularly to see how they are progressing and offers advice on how they can unlock their potential. He is personally focused on ensuring that each individual achieves their fitness goals in an injury-free manner.

When Jatin speaks or presents, his executive presence is automatically great because he is dedicated to the purpose of helping others. His passion drives his ability to communicate in an inspiring manner!

Use Depth to Drive Dedication

Here is an interesting point: dedication drives depth. Dedicated individuals take efforts to increase their depth. However, sometimes you can also enhance your depth to enhance your dedication!

Here is a story to explain this: A few years ago, I was having a conversation with an entrepreneur. He was facing a unique challenge. He wanted his team to be focused on the customer and wanted them to arrive at a strong customer value proposition. However, he was struggling to inspire his team on this and was not able to work with them to articulate the organization's differentiated value proposition.

As our conversation progressed, I asked him a simple question: "How much data do you have to understand customer needs and expectations?" He was honest in his answer that, though they had access to some quantitative data, they did not have access to real customer feelings about the brand. We agreed that there was a knowledge gap that had to be plugged.

I explained to him the interlinkage of depth and dedication. We discussed what he can do to first increase his depth on customer expectations and feelings. As a result of brainstorming, we identified a few actions:

- He would speak with 100 customers himself over the next few months to understand how they perceive the brand.

- The organisation would engage a market research organisation to develop a better understanding of customer perception versus competition.

- He would use the above to shape his point of view and messaging.

When we met a few months later, the situation had significantly improved. Because he had invested time to increase his own depth, he was much more confident about customer needs and expectations. He had strategic clarity on differentiation, value proposition, and his personal excitement had enhanced. He had become more mission-oriented.

By increasing his depth, he had unlocked his dedication. He had realized that value proportion is not just a set of features, but an overall brand promise to positively impact the lives of customers.

His newfound understanding was also now being translated into more inspiring messages for his team. They could "feel the desired customer experience" in the way he spoke, and gradually, the naysayers were converting to adopters.

So, next time, when you are finding it hard to uncover your own dedication, try to develop deeper depth in an area. It just works!

As a summary, if you are trying to develop your own dedication, try to ask yourself the following questions:

- Do others perceive me as a dedicated leader? If not, what can I do to change that?

- What are those 1-2 areas that I am passionate and dedicated about?

- What can I do to uncover dedication for a purpose or dedication for helping others?

- Which out of these four practices can I intentionally deploy?

  - Uncover superordinate goals.

  - Paint a picture of the future.

- ○ Focus on helping others.

- ○ Use depth to drive dedication.

Down To Earth

The final key character trait of executive presence is about humility, i.e., how "down to earth" the person we are listening to is.

During the course of my consulting career, I have met many leaders who have the depth and the dedication, but they are not down to earth. These leaders inspire, but in a very limited manner.

At the start of this book, I mentioned 2 questions about executive presence:

1. How do listeners feel about the communicator during and at the end of communication?

2. How do listeners feel about themselves during and after the communication?

When a speaker is down to earth, they have a positive impact on both of these experiences.

A few years ago, I had a chance to attend a presentation from a senior leader of a large organization. This speaker had all going for him from the perspective of executive presence. He had amazing mastery over his subject and was extremely dedicated to the topic.

His ability to articulate his thoughts was perfect, and his entire presentation was full of brilliant delivery techniques. However, he was extremely arrogant.

During the entire meeting, he had an air of "I know better" around him. Several times during the meeting, participants felt that he was talking down to them. There was an air of uneasiness during and after his presentation.

During a coffee break that followed, there were murmurs in conversations that this individual was "too much in love with himself."

When we think about inspiration, it is the process of being mentally stimulated to do something. The only thing that this speaker was able to inspire was what should not be done!

Down to earth individuals inspire in a very different manner. Through their humility, learning attitude, and role model behaviors, they inspire the listeners' "whole self." They are able to appeal to a very basic human requirement – Respect.

Leaders with humility display the following behaviors when they speak:

- While they share good ideas themselves, they are open to listening to ideas from the listeners.

- They operate with a lifelong learning approach after having realized that *depth is not attained; it is constantly sought.*

- They are authentically curious to get perspectives from others on their ideas and, if needed, adapt their solutions when they notice logical arguments.

- They raise the self-esteem of the listeners in the way they treat them.

- They realize the role that humility has played in their success and consciously strive to remain humble.

I am better than others

One of the key issues that blocks humility is the internal script that many people can have – "I am better than others." When we constantly run this narrative in our own mind, we actually start looking at others with arrogance (and sometimes disdain). This starts coming out in the way we speak and the "signals" we send through our communication.

Unfortunately, many people can live this narrative unconsciously, and they can get trapped in a frustrating cycle when others don't respond accordingly. It requires deep self-awareness and courage to acknowledge this and transform yourself on this matter.

We notice people wearing the "I am better than others" label all the time. We see them in meetings, on social media, during events, and over emails!

Sometimes, it can be quite puzzling as to why people fall into this trap. People can sometimes lose sight of the fact that if they have done well in their professional life, it can be a factor of many things, including:

- Their capability,

- Opportunities given to them.

- Ecosystem,

- Their mentors.

- Positive market.

- And sometimes, just pure luck!

Therefore, it's a pertinent question to ask ourselves: When people experience me, do they experience a humble individual or an arrogant one?

Power of Operating Principles to Enhance Humility

One of the key questions that I get asked is, can people who are arrogant learn to be humble? Absolutely, yes, they can!

However, this requires courage and operating principles. Let me explain this through the help of an example.

A few years ago, I was coaching a leader who was trapped in the world of "I am better than others." This was destroying his relationships at work, creating stress at home, and diluting his leadership brand. This person used to head the strategy function of a large organization, and specifically, the following things were happening:

- During strategy planning and review meetings, he used to approach his peers with the mindset of "they are not good enough."

- Whenever any strategic initiative was a success, he used to attribute it to himself and wanted to be the centre of attention.

- Most of his conversations with the CEO were a list of complaints about how people in the organisation were not good or issues with the organisation.

Because of the above, most of his peers avoided getting into a conversation with him. Whenever an issue used to happen, they used to worry about the messaging he would give to the CEO. This led them to over-justify their own stance.

The CEO himself saw a huge potential in this leader, but started avoiding meetings with him because he found them "mentally draining."

At the start of our coaching engagement, we conducted a 360-degree assessment, and the results were quite telling. The results had an emotional impact on the Strategy Head. As it generally happens, his initial reaction to the 360-degree was quite defensive. He felt that his peers were "out to get him" and that they were jealous of his success.

However, as the conversations progressed, I requested this leader to think authentically about the results and ask himself whether there were parts of the feedback that he accepted. I also asked him to consider what parts of his behavior contributed to the feedback.

Fortunately, after a very candid conversation, he started agreeing with the fact that he was approaching people with some degree of arrogance, and he also started realizing that for him to grow, he would need to develop higher levels of humility.

He asked for guidance on how he could improve on this. This is when I shared with him the concept of operating principles. Simply put, "operating principles are the way we get things done." It comprises a list of values, behaviors, and principles that help us to operate. When identified well, they become a guiding light on how to work.

As I explained the concept to him, I asked him to think about operating principles from the perspective of arrogance and humility. I asked him to make a list of his current operating principles that were making him work in an arrogant manner. He made a very powerful list, comprising the following: My current operating principles are:

- I feel that I am the best.

- When issues happen, I feel it is because of others.

- Getting feedback can make me angry.

I then requested him to imagine that he was a down-to-earth, humble leader. With that vision in mind, I asked him to consider what his operating principles "should be." This is the list that he generated:

- I am good at what I do, but I can learn more.

- When issues occur, think objectively about what caused them.

- Notice the strengths of others.

- Pause and think before responding to a disagreement.

Once he had identified these principles, then came the most important step. I requested him to consider that these operating principles are behaviors he needs to practice daily! Unless he consciously implements them daily, he will go like a rubber band into dysfunctional behaviors.

We agreed that he would maintain a log of this, and we decided to review his progress periodically. The results were extraordinary! We saw a major change in him within one month of starting this process.

His colleagues, though initially skeptical, welcomed the new person, and his personal stress levels went down. Over a period of 6 months, this leader went on to build several collaborative relationships in his organization.

Here are some "generic" operating principles that I have found helpful to develop conscious humility:

- Be a lifelong learner, approach every meeting with a learning mindset.

- Consciously focus on the strengths of others.

- Attribute issues to context, rather than people.

- Solve problems by developing processes, rather than attacking people.

- Be open to change and feedback.

- Share credit for personal achievements.

In case you are trying to develop humility, some of these can offer a helpful start.

If you would like to know how humble you currently are, here is a quick self-assessment you can do to answer this question:

Humility Self-Assessment

Take a few minutes to conduct the self-assessment below. Rate yourself on a scale of 1 to 5 for each statement. Scale:

5-Strongly Agree

4-Agree

3-Neither Agree nor Disagree.

2-Disagree

1-Strongly Disagree

During a presentation or a meeting:	5	4	3	2	1
I listen actively when others share their views and ideas.					
I am open to considering new ideas, irrespective of where they come from.					
I don't let my subject matter expertise convert into arrogance.					
I am willing to admit when I have not explored a nuance that others point out.					
I express gratitude to others and share the spotlight with them, if needed.					
I avoid talking down to others.					
I showcase genuine curiosity to learn from others.					
I adequately balance the amount of time I am talking versus the amount of time I am listening.					
I don't react negatively when people disagree with me.					
I create an environment in which others feel comfortable in sharing their views					

Putting the 3 Ds Together

Now, that we have a common understanding of the 3Ds, it will be clear that all of these 3 are critical. In fact, each of them is linked to the other 2.

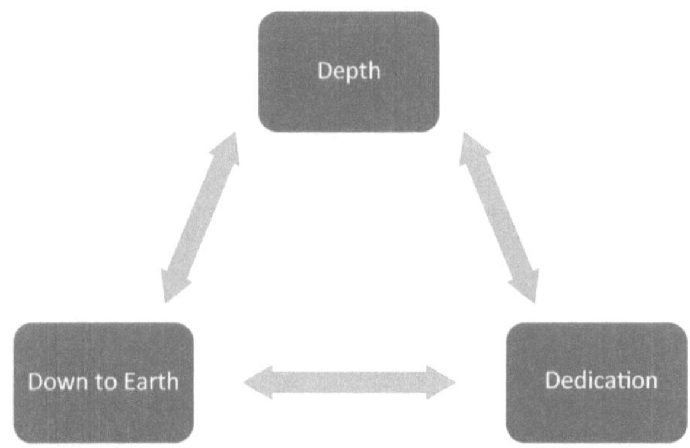

An individual who is down-to-earth showcases "humble inquiry" to pursue depth. This humility also drives their dedication to help and support others.

Pursuit of depth requires dedication and a lifelong learning attitude, which requires humility. Similarly, when we are dedicated to a task/ purpose, it drives us to explore the depth more and makes us appreciate the talent in our chosen field.

Ask yourself again, "How do others experience me from the lens of 3Ds?" Identify that one D that you can focus more on, develop, and execute a sincere plan to implement, and let the magic begin!

Summary

- The dictionary definition of depth is the "distance between the surface and bottom of anything." When talking about a topic, it means how much we really know and understand it.

- While leaders with strong executive presence can use tips and techniques to deliver their message more effectively, these techniques are not a replacement for their depth (or lack of it).

- Depth does not mean static knowledge, i.e., understanding a particular area or a concept at one time, but it means adopting a lifelong learning attitude to explore that area further.

- People with depth display the following behaviours:

  - Realize that knowing a concept is just the start. It is continuous exploration, which is the key.

  - Take out structured time for reflection. These individuals objectively assess themselves.

  - Spend a lot of time reading about their chosen area. Invest time in going deeper by constantly acquiring new knowledge and skills.

  - Naturally inclined toward outside-in thinking, i.e., linking new, unrelated items to their area of expertise.

  - Adopt a "learn-it-all" mindset.

- To increase depth, focus on the 6 levels of expertise framework.

- Dedicated individuals are special; they have

  - An inherent sense of purpose drives them.

  - Infectious magnetic energy that draws people to them.

  - Passion that inspires others to act.

- From the perspective of executive presence, dedication comes in two types:

  - Dedication to a task/purpose.

  - Dedication to help and support others.

- To unlock dedication, apply these two practices:

  - Uncover superordinate goals.

  - Paint a picture of the future.

  - Focus on helping others.

  - Use depth to drive dedication.

- The final key character trait of executive presence is about humility, i.e., how "down to earth" the person we are listening to is.

- Down-to-earth individuals inspire in a very different manner. Through their humility, learning attitude, and role model behaviors, they inspire the listeners' "whole self." They are able to appeal to a very basic human requirement – Respect.

- Down to earth, requires humility as a leader.

- Avoid an "I am better than others" mindset to prevent arrogance and enhance humility.

- Use the power of operating principles to enhance humility. Some key operating principles to consider include:

  - Be a lifelong learner, approach every meeting with a learning mindset.

  - Consciously focus on the strengths of others.

  - Attribute issues to context, rather than people.

  - Solve problems by developing processes, rather than attacking people.

  - Be open to change and feedback.

  - Share credit for personal achievements.

- Depth, Dedication, and Down to Earth are all inter-related.

- Ask yourself, "How do others experience me from the lens of 3Ds?" Identify that one D that you can focus more on.

Part 5

My AURA Action Plan

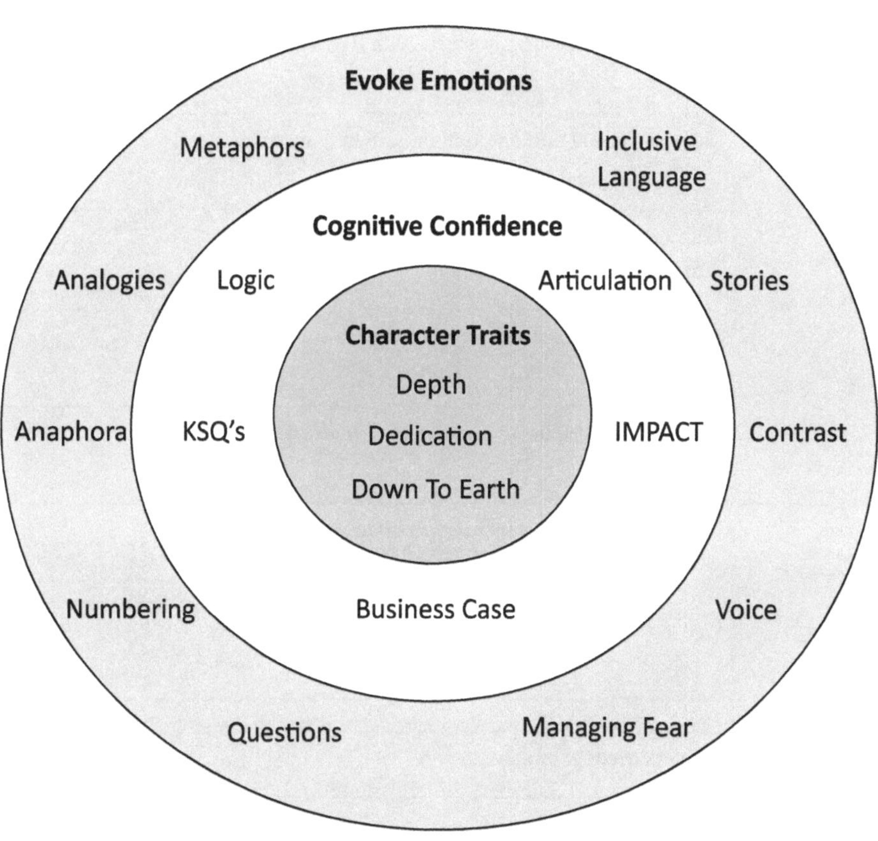

Your Action Plan

Now that we have explored the concept of AURA in detail, here is an integrated assessment and action planning tool for you.

Part 1: Ability to Build Cognitive Confidence

On the statements below, rate yourself on a scale of 1 to 5. Use 5 if you are very good in this area and 1 if you have a lot to improve on.

Dimension	Statement	Rating (1-5)
Precise Articulation.	When I communicate, my articulation is precise.	
	Most people will find my communication to be crisp.	
	I stay on the topic of discussion and avoid going off in different, unrelated dimensions.	
	Most people tell me that I am very clear in communication.	
	I don't find myself needing to explain my idea repetitively.	
Logic	I find it easy to make other people understand my logic or rationale.	
	I am able to provide relevant facts and details as needed.	
	I can easily define the problem statements and why the problem needs to be solved.	
	When developing ideas, I consider multiple alternatives and carefully assess the pros and cons of my ideas.	
	I proactively identify risk areas to develop practical ideas.	

Part 2: Evoking emotions through communication techniques

Reflect on the 10 communication techniques below, and rate yourself as per the scale below:

3: I am an expert in this; it comes naturally to me.

2: I am okay in this, but I need to become better.

1: This is a technique I need to consciously attempt and practice more.

Communication Technique	Rating (1-3)	One thing I can consciously do to improve in this, if needed,
Metaphors		
Analogies		
Anaphora		
Numbering		
Questions with strategic pauses,		
Inclusive language.		
Storytelling		
Contrast		
Voice Modulation		
Managing Butterflies		

Part 3: Character- Depth, Dedication and Down To Earth

On the statements below, rate yourself on a scale of 1 to 5. Use 5 if you are very good in this area and 1 if you have a lot to improve on.

Dimension	Statement	Rating (1-5)
Depth	I have a reasonable depth in my focus area.	
	I invest reasonable time in going deeper (in my focus area) by constantly acquiring new knowledge and skills.	
	I am naturally inclined toward outside-in thinking, i.e., linking new, unrelated items to my area of expertise.	
	Most people will describe me as a lifelong learner.	
Dedication	I have an inherent purpose that drives me.	
	I focused on helping and supporting others.	
	When people speak with me, they can sense that they are talking to a dedicated and passionate individual.	
	My passion inspires others to act.	
Down to Earth	Most people would describe me as someone with humility.	
	I don't operate with an "I am best" mindset.	
	When successful, I am conscious of sharing credit with others.	
	I don't get overly focused on weaknesses of others.	

Part 4: My AURA Action Plan: Basis Above, Put a Tick Against Areas Below on Which You Can Improve

Component	Sub Component	Tick if applicable.
Cognitive Confidence.	Logical thinking	
	Precise articulation.	
Communication Techniques	Metaphors	
	Analogies	
	Anaphora	
	Numbering	
	Questions with strategic pauses,	
	Inclusive language.	
	Storytelling	
	Contrast	
	Voice Modulation	
	Managing Butterflies	
Character	Depth	
	Dedication	
	Down to Earth	

Part 4: My AURA Action Plan: Continued

Create your AURA action plan below

Component	Which parameter/s can you improve on?	Identify 3-4 actions you will take to improve yourself. See tools and frameworks checklist on next page for reference.
Cognitive Confidence		
Communication Techniques		
Character		

Quick Reference Guide: Tools and Frameworks

This reference guide covers all the key tools, tips, and frameworks covered in this book. Use it as a personal development toolkit.

Component	Tool/Framework	Purpose	Page Number
Cognitive Confidence.	1. Logic articulation matrix.	Evaluate where you are in this matrix.	22
	2. Key Stakeholder Questions.	Use this framework to prepare for communication.	26
	3. Business Case Thinker.	Evaluate whether you are a business case thinker or a single idea thinker.	30
	4. IMPACT Framework.	Integrated framework to connect KSQs with Business Case	37
	5. Self-awareness tool for over-explaining.	Use this tool to find out reasons why people over-explain.	42
Communication Vehicles	6. Guidelines for developing metaphors.	Use these practices to develop metaphors.	53
	7. Tell, Explain, Leverage	3-step framework to develop analogies	58
	8. Practical tips to use anaphora.	Use as a checklist for anaphora.	65
	9. Numbering Exercise.	Leverage this exercise to use numbering.	71
	10. Inclusive language self-assessment.	Use this to self-assess your language.	85
	11. S.T.O.R.Y.	Tool to develop and use stories.	88
	12. Using contrast.	Practical tips to leverage contrasts.	95
	13. Cognitive distortions assessment.	Use this assessment to check your cognitive distortions.	104
	14. Mind Mapping.	Leverage this technique to memorize your presentation.	109

Component	Tool/Framework	Purpose	Page Number
Character	15. Four quadrant framework for depth.	Use this tool to enhance your depth.	119
	16. Levels of expertise.	Leverage this framework to assess your current level of expertise.	123
	17. Practices to unlock dedication.	4 techniques to unlock your own dedication.	127
	18. Humility self-assessment.	Leverage this assessment to check your humility quotient.	139